MONEY RAISING AND PLANNING FOR THE SMALL BUSINESS

MONEY RAISING AND PLANNING FOR THE SMALL BUSINESS

David L. Markstein

HENRY REGNERY COMPANY•Chicago

Library of Congress Cataloging in Publication Data
Markstein, David L.
  Money raising and planning for the small business.
  1. Small business—United States—Finance.
I. Title.
HG3729.U5M35   658.1'522   73-18123

Published by Henry Regnery Company
114 West Illinois Street, Chicago, Illinois 60610
Manufactured in the United States of America
Library of Congress Catalog Card Number: 73-18123
International Standard Book Number: 0-8092-9075-8

To my Aunt Sadie Markstein,
an indomitable and wonderful lady

Contents

MONEY RAISING AND PLANNING FOR THE SMALL BUSINESS

1: Who Has the Money You Need?

THE big operator can raise whatever money he needs. If he wants to raise funds to start a new business or obtain money for expansion, he gets it because he has position and knows where to go and whom to see. But heaven help the little guy who needs capital.

Do you believe that's true? If so, you find yourself in the majority. You are also dead wrong.

You're wrong, first, in believing that big operators always get the money they need. Receivers for the ailing giant Penn Central, a staggering, reeling company with thousands of miles of potentially profitable railroad tracks and some of the juciest parcels of property in midtown New York, can tell you differently. So can officials of many big brokerage companies that, despite impeccable Wall Street connections, went broke in the crunch of the early seventies. Big operators don't always have it easy when they require capital.

Nor do little fellows always have it tough. There are more avenues open for the borrowing and raising of capital for a

1

new small business than for many big business ventures whose very size and bulk makes their needs hard to fill.

This book tells you how to raise capital—where to go, whom to see, and what to say to him, where the money is and the keys to unlocking it. It's knowledge that all businessmen—even established ones—need, because study after study has shown that more small-to-medium businesses fail through inadequate capitalization and from lack of sufficient day-to-day working capital than from any other cause. It's needless failure.

You can do something about the problem. You can act to get a bank loan at cheaper rates. This book will tell you how to do it. You can move to secure more permanent means of financing. Later chapters will tell you how to do that, too. You can look up the people other than bankers who supply funds to businesses and individuals and learn the ways they operate. The book will tell you that also.

Even for people who aren't in the position of small-businessman-in-need-of-funds-but-scared-of-extending-today's-high-interest-rates-over-years-to-come, the matter of borrowing at least cost is important. It comes up if you want to buy a car, finance a trip to photograph wild life in Africa or fish in Alaska, or just borrow something to whoop it up at the corner bar. The cheaper you can get the money, the better.

Borrowed money can make money.

Let's repeat that: *Borrowed money can make money.*

For you. Now. Later chapters will tell you how.

The first chapter of a how-you-can-do-it book is usually designed to get people into the tent where, in later chapters, they can be exposed to the arguments and explanations of the author. This book is no exception. What follows here is to get you into the tent and to start you—whether you're a big businessman, little operator, professional person, or anyone else who from time to time needs to employ the money of others and who in these days of taut money and stringent interest rates finds the high cost of money a handicap—going into ways you can beat that handicap. In the right circumstances, you can even turn it into an advantage. You can't escape high interest or other costs altogether, but you can render them less crippling.

The subject, then, is *money*, how to get it as cheaply and plentifully as possible and how to lend or otherwise put it to work for the biggest return possible.

So the first step is to look at the stuff we're going to be talking about in the next eleven chapters—money. Let's let the expert tell it. Hear what the Federal Reserve Bank of Richmond said in a booklet called *Readings on Money*:

> It has been said that the economic health of the nation rests essentially on faith, since virtually every transaction that takes place involves trust and confidence. This is true because the prerequisite of every transaction—the means of making payment—is itself a form of credit. Furthermore, every delayed payment is in essence credit, and a very substantial portion of all payments is delayed. The employee who receives payment for his services at the end of a period of service, the electric company that bills for power supplied in a past period, the supplier who bills the manufacturer for raw material after delivery—each has surrendered services or commodities on trust, with the faith, although buttressed by the force of law, that payment will be satisfied in the normal course of economic events.
>
> Few pause to consider the magnitude of merely the more easily recognized forms of credit. An individual borrows money from his bank in order to purchase a home, an automobile, a refrigerator, a power mower. A retail merchant makes a loan to purchase inventory. A manufacturer procures money from the public by selling bonds. The United States government borrows by issuing and selling bonds, notes, certificates of indebtedness, or bills. In each case borrower and lender are easily recognized. The total amount owed by all borrowers at the end of 1966 was estimated by the Department of Commerce at $1,346 billion.

This was 81 percent greater than the nation's gross national product—the market value of all goods and services produced —in the United States in that year.

For every borrower there must be a lender. This raises the query: Who are the lenders of money and what is the source of the money they lend? Initially we might say simply that loan-able funds come either from money already in use but not being spent by its owners (that is, savings, past or present) or from money newly created by the lending process. The loan contract is the instrument not only for transporting idle funds from savers to those who can put them to current use but also for bringing into existence entirely new funds which are put to work and exert their influence, at times profound influence, on the economy.

In the present intricate economic structure, painfully evolved through centuries of trial and error, the saver of funds rarely comes into contact with the borrower. He deposits his funds in a savings account, pays an insurance premium, purchases shares in a savings and loan association, or contributes to a pension fund—in these and other ways he puts his funds in the hands of a financial middleman. The financial middleman then seeks to employ them in such a manner that he is always ready to meet demands made upon him by the savers who entrusted their funds to him, to pay them the agreed rate of return for the use of the money, and also to acquire a profit to the institution above the cost of its operation.

.   This generally smooth-working process of putting saved funds to work has important economic implications. It means that the saving of present income for future use need not cause a reduction in the overall level of spending currently taking place. It means also that saving becomes profitable, that saved funds can be put to work in earning a return for their owners, thus providing an additional incentive to save.

There are many kinds of lenders, the Richmond Fed pointed out, and each has a way of doing business. Knowing the roles of these can be helpful in finding new avenues when Banker Paul slaps that 9½ percent quote on you and a cup of coffee—even a scotch and water—fails to make the wound less painful or crippling. Loan sources, said the Fed, include the **institutional lenders.**

In the complex American economy there are a great number of institutions whose primary function revolves around the borrowing and lending of money. Some of these act as true middlemen—they receive funds from savers, the ultimate lenders, and on their own initiative and judgment lend these funds to a vast array of borrowers constantly seeking present use of their future income. Among them are specialists in the financial services they offer, as, for example, sales finance companies, consumer finance companies, and credit unions, which lend almost entirely to individuals for purposes of personal consumption, or savings and loan associations and mutual savings banks, which invest most of their available funds in mortgage loans.

Other financial middlemen offer a much broader service and cater to almost all classes of loan demand. Included in this group are the commercial banks, whose borrowers range from farmers to home owners, from individual consumers to business firms—the pygmy-sized as well as the corporate giants. Their investment portfolios include bonds of a varied assortment of corporate enterprises as well as obligations of the United States government and of states and political subdivisions.

The Federal Reserve study noted that **commercial banks**

differ from all others by an extremely important attribute: Their demand deposit credit is money and need not be converted into some other form to be used in buying and selling. Commercial banks can, therefore, lend their own credit, whereas other lenders must make payment to their borrowers in the form of currency or of bank demand deposit money. Other lenders are restricted in their lending to the actual money they have at their command, while commercial banks may, within certain limits, create the funds—their own demand deposit credit—that they lend.

The limits to deposit expansion are set by legally-required reserves, which, in effect, set the amount of reserves the banking system must retain for each dollar of bank credit extended. Thus, with a given amount of reserves, the banking system can extend several times that amount of credit to its customers.

Bank lending is both broader in scope and greater in total amount than that of any other type of financial institution. Over 60 percent of all the loans and investments held by the principal lenders are owned by commercial banks. Their lending ranges in maturity from one or two days (for example, Federal funds loaned to another bank to meet a temporary need) to twenty-five or thirty years, as in the case of VA guaranteed mortgage loans or certain long-term bonds. Their borrowing customers may be consumers, farmers, home buyers, retail or wholesale merchants, construction firms, manufacturing and mining concerns, and many others, including other financial institutions borrowing in order to be able to meet demands of their own borrowing customers. Commercial banks are truly the department stores of the financial field.

Insurance companies lend in big amounts, generally for longer periods than do banks. Classified by the Richmond Federal Reserve Bank's writers as institutional lenders, the insurance giants

> also offer an extremely variegated credit service. Their lending practices differ from those of the commercial banks in that more of their loan and investment assets are acquired in the financial markets, although there are many direct lender-borrower transactions. Their loans to business and industry include vast amounts of corporate bonds and stocks purchased in the market as well as many direct purchases and a large number of individual loan transactions. Even home mortgages are purchased in large blocks in the secondary market, but in this type of lending there are also many direct home buyer-lender transactions. At the end of 1966, almost half of the credit

extended by life insurance companies was in the form of securities of the federal government or of the states and their political subdivisions.

A major source of life insurance companies' investment funds is from policy holders. In recent years premium income has provided about one-half of the total, the remaining half coming from earnings on investments, income from rental properties, and other sources.

In the old American tradition are the **mutual savings banks**, "owned," the Fed noted,

and operated for the benefit of their depositor members. Loanable funds are derived almost entirely from the savings of members, and earnings are shared on a mutual basis. Earnings, which are retained to provide appropriate reserves and for other purposes, provide a second source of funds to the savings banks.

Credit policies of the mutual savings banks are traditionally conservative, and every effort is made to reduce the risk element in their investments to a minimum. Mortgage loans provide their principal lending outlet, and these include mortgages on commercial properties as well as those on homes. Their other assets are almost entirely in the form of government securities and the higher grade public utility and industrial bonds.

Most (not all) **savings and loan associations** are like mutual banks in that they are owned and run for members. Some are stock companies, especially in the West, and among these are a few big operators with shares listed on the New York Stock Exchange and possessed of nearly as many offices as the Bank of America or Macy's. The S & L's concentrate upon lending in the building field, mostly in mortgage financing of home construction and the purchase of older homes. There is a difference between ownership of S & L associations and ownership of a regular corporation with nonpublicly traded stock. S & L capital is withdrawable, and in the severe 1969 credit crunch many owners did take away their funds to put them into better-paying bonds, notes, and Treasury bills. There now appears to be a flow back to the old savings and loan homestead on the downtown of Gravel and Pitt from which so many of us financed our first home ownership. According to the Federal Reserve, savings and loan societies furnish funds for more home mortgages than any other lending source.

There are the **sales finance companies**, which put money into refrigerator, automobile, TV, and other relatively small purchases people make. According to the experts from the Richmond Federal Reserve Bank, these

are the only important institutional lenders in our economy that do not rely upon the savings of a large number of individuals as their principal source of funds. An important margin of their loanable funds is derived from their owners' equity. In addition to owners' equity, which represents paid-in capital plus retained earnings, these companies provide themselves with a substantial amount of working funds by borrowing from banks, insurance companies, and other institutional investors. In addition, the larger companies frequently sell their own short-term notes in the open market.

The sales finance companies have grown up with the automobile. Loans for financing the purchase of automobiles account for the major portion of the business handled by them. Although these companies handle consumer-type loans almost exclusively, they are to be distinguished from other consumer credit institutions in that they deal primarily with . . . consumer durable goods dealers rather than with the consumer. They, in effect, purchase installment notes or credit instruments in other forms from the dealers who have themselves arranged the credit purchase with the customer.

Finally, there are lending sources such as the credit union, the consumer loan company whose "Friendly Joe" (or Pete,

Sam, Bob, Pat, Hans, Ian, Ivan, Sean, Jean, Juan, or whoever) beams from the newspaper ad as he offers to all comers
small bundles of cash at usually large interest costs. "In
addition," concluded the Federal Reserve study, there are
"mortgage companies, stock savings banks, industrial banks,
trust companies, and cash depositories. In addition to the
multitude of private lenders, a number of government
agencies are active in the lending field. Among their borrowers are farmers, financial institutions, exporters and im-
porters, and foreign governments."

The Fed's study summarizes the kinds of lending sources.
It does not tell—as the present work will—the sources of more
permanent money, such as the people engaged in placing
venture capital, the mutual funds and others seeking letter
stock, the underwriters, and specialized bankers who function
more as sellers than lenders.

Nor does the Fed study tell you how to approach the
lenders it lists. A coming chapter will examine pointers for
getting close to prime rate instead of high interest. We will
explore how different collateral can change an answer from
no to *yes* when you want to borrow at small cost, and we will
look at traps formed by the seemingly innocuous words *discount* and *compensating balance*.

Another chapter might be the most important piece of
reading you will do this year. It looks at leasing as a means of
financing everything from lands and buildings to the car you
drive to work. Leasing is no cure-all. It has many drawbacks
along with its advantages. We will examine when a lease deal
is profitable and how to judge when it might work out to be a
high-cost, rather than low-cost, method of financing.

Mortgages are the conventional method for financing real
estate. A mortgage can be expensive, and on occasion dis-
astrous, if you don't know what you're doing or are unaware
of the ways you can rewrite certain standard clauses to make
sure that high interest costs won't linger on when the days of
low interest come back. That's the content of a coming chapter,

along with advice on how to negotiate a land or building lease (itself a method of financing or of freeing capital for other uses) without hobbling yourself with restrictions and probable future lawsuits.

Today, both sizable and small institutions search out firms (like yours?) into which to invest venture capital. The field is growing and the idea is popular. But you won't obtain the benefits of low-cost financing from this source unless you know how. The key is given in a following chapter.

Uncle Sam offers all kinds of help. In another coming chapter you will look over the agencies that lend, give, invest, and supply money; what conditions they demand; and how to negotiate for capital obtainable at rates as low, in some cases, as 2 percent.

Your own investment portfolio can furnish the capital for other ventures if you handle options instead of stock in order to turn investment capital into free operating funds. If you follow rules recommended and ideas put forth, your investment results actually can improve through lessening of the amount invested. Paradoxical but possible, as many who have tried this method know.

You must know the economic climate and the probabilities of future rain or sunshine. An "in" idea for forecasting business conditions is the use of leading, coincident, and lagging indicators exhaustively studied by the National Bureau of Economic Research. These are available to you at a cost of only $16 per year if you follow instructions. Rapidly replacing Keynesian economics among the newer breed of financial crystal ballers is the monetary approach pioneered by such economists as Milton Friedman of the University of Chicago and Darryl Francis, president of the Federal Reserve Bank of St. Louis. Their methods can be in your hands for study each week so your timing will be right.

To recap:
1. In a time of high-cost money, with big, prime borrowers paying big interest, you have little chance to obtain a loan at

even the prohibitive rate and no chance at all of getting it by conventional methods at a better rate. But there are unconvential ways.

2. The search for money at reasonable rates begins with an understanding of who are the lenders and what field each lender covers—how he does his thing.

3. Lenders aren't the only sources of funds. Money can be obtained from governmental agencies, venture capitalists, seekers of letter stock bargains, and other suppliers of capital. Unsophisticated business and professional people rarely know about these sources.

4. The money thus obtained can be put to work in a variety of long-term and short-term ways designed to make the money you have secured at low cost work for you to generate high returns.

5. The chapters that follow will detail such offbeat sources, what they want from you, and what you can reasonably expect from them.

2: Forecasting Financial Needs

An old adage says that it is not what you know that counts, but who. In obtaining new capital, when is an important factor.

During good times, it is easy to borrow money, and you can put it to use more easily. During recessionary periods—these come despite efforts of government and business to iron out the peaks and valleys—money is harder to find, and it is often expensive to borrow. When you can find it, you pay a lot to get it, and when you put it to work, you often find profits harder to come by.

This can be summed up in one sentence: Those who swim with the economic current find their going easier than those who swim against it.

Therefore, you've got to form some working idea of what is coming in the period ahead so that you can maximize the good times when jobs are plentiful, factories hum, stores are busy, the chances for a new business to succeed are very high, and money is generally easy. Money costs very little then compared to the high interest rates and tough terms encountered during recessionary and near-recessionary periods.

It is not hard to tell when you are in such a happy era. But how long will it last, and will it still be around by the time your plans mature? If you're in a tight money period, when will the good days begin again?

You don't have to be an economist to make this determination. You do have to put in some minimum study. It won't be as exciting as a party or as relaxing as a Sunday picnic, but it can pay off bigger.

Writing on "Money, Interest Rates, Prices, and Output" in the St. Louis Federal Reserve Bank's *Monthly Review*, Jerry L. Jordan of the bank's staff noted:

> In financial markets interest rates are the prices at which quantity supplied and quantity demanded of particular financial assets are equated. The way in which money stock is related to the demand for any supply of some financial assets is somewhat complex. On the one hand, an increase in the money supply and bank credit adds directly to the supply of lendable funds. An increase in money results in the bidding up of the prices of financial assets, causing interest rates to be lower than they otherwise would be.
>
> On the other hand, some argue that a rise in the money supply and bank credit also has expansionary effects on the total demand for goods and services. If dollar balances and credit are increased rapidly, given existing assets, incomes, prices, and interest rates, people will attempt to exchange the excess money for goods, services, or other financial assets. Any increase in the demand for goods and services will result initially in the running down of inventories and subsequently a rise in production and an increase in credit demands. . . . If the rates of increase in money supply, credit, and total demand are faster than the rates at which output can be increased, prices will rise. Rising prices will cause increased demands for credit, since more funds are needed to finance a given volume of goods. With expectations of inflation, borrowers are willing to

pay higher rates since they expect to repay with cheaper dollars, and lenders charge higher rates in order to net the same real return in the process of allocating limited funds.

An older and still extremely accurate method of forecasting turns from boom conditions to bust conditions, and from the shadows and gloom of a recession into the bright sunlight of new good times, is by use of the leading indicators.

These are among the wealth of available economic data series. The National Bureau of Economic Research pioneered the study of these series. Its study separated them into leading, coincident, and lagging series. The first group tends to bottom out and start upward *in advance* of the whole economy. The second group moves *with* the economy. And the third group moves *behind* the economy.

"It's as if you were in a moving automobile," one economist who has studied these series told me. "The leading series are like a look through the front windshield. They tell you where you are headed. Examining the second group is like looking out of the side windows. You get a view of where you are. Checking into the third group is something like looking through the back window of the car. You can see where you have been."

What counts for us, seeking to know the coming economic climate, is the group of leading indicators. Let the expert tell it. Writing in the magazine *Financial Analysts Journal*, Jesse Levin, an economic statistician, noted in the July-August 1970 issue:

> Probably the least understood tools of financial analysis are the leading indicators of the National Bureau of Economic Research. The NBER is a non-profit organization upon which the U.S. Department of Commerce depends for the many business statistics it releases periodically in its publication *Business Conditions Digest*. Between the members of the executive board and the staff statisticians there are at all times a large

number of experts studying every phase of the economy and tracing the relationships among various business statistics, which they call *indicators*. In the over thirty years that they have been conducting these studies, the NBER economists have reached some important conclusions regarding the relative timing with which these indicators reach their high and low points in every business cycle.

They have found, for instance, that in changes of trend certain business indicators always precede the general economy. These indicators usually reach their peaks and then head downward months before the trend of general business turns down. In the midst of most recessions, they turn around and head upward while the economy is still dropping. Because they forewarn of approaching downturns and upturns in the economy, NBER economists have labelled these indicators "Leading Indicators of Business." At present they classify thirty-six indicators as leading. Within the past two years, they selected a short list of twelve indicators that produce the same result as the larger group. Recently they have reported monthly figures for a composite of the twelve leaders, including numbers:

1. average work week
6. new orders, durable goods industries
10. contracts and orders, plant and equipment
16. corporate profits after tax
17. ratio, price to unit labor cost, manufacturing
19. stock prices, 500 stocks
23. industrial materials prices
29. building permits, private housing
30. non-agricultural placements, all industries
31. change in book value, manufacturing and trade industries
38. index of net business formations
113. change in consumer installment debt

The NBER classifies another group of indicators as "Coincident Indicators of Business" because they have found, over the year, that these directly measure *current* aggregate economic activity. Among these are such statistics as industrial production and retail sales. Although there are now twenty-five such coin-

cident indicators, the short list contains but seven, including numbers:
   41. employees in non-agricultural establishments
   43. total unemployment rate (inverted)
   47. industrial production
   50. Gross National Product in 1958 dollars
   52. personal income
   54. sales of retail stores
  816. manufacturing and trade sales

The classification of indicators as leading, coincident, or lagging is based primarily on their relative timing in past economic cycles. But there is also a logical reason for their classification. For instance, when business slows down, an employer does not like to break up an experienced organization when he can avoid it by first putting his force on part time. Conversely, when business improves, the employer prefers to put his force on overtime, rather than break in untrained help, until he is certain he can no longer avoid doing so. For this reason, average work week precedes unemployment.

A similar logical sequence exists between new orders for durable goods and industrial production. From 1949 to 1967, new orders reached trend change points ahead of production seven times out of seven (not including ties).

The National Bureau classifies five other indicators as lagging indicators because they have usually lagged behind the economy in their trend changes. Some will be surprised to learn that expenditures for new plant and equipment is not a forecaster, but rather a lagger.

In 1965, I tried to find a short list of four leading indicators that would give the same advance warning as the larger group. Using data for the period 1948-1961 I tried out these four: 500 stocks, average work week, new orders for durable goods, and private non-farm housing starts, and compared their relative timing vis à vis the economy and each other.

During slumps in business, common stocks generally turn up before most leading indicators of this group. This is not surprising since it is generally believed that stocks forecast coming business. However, in *every* period of expansion from 1948 to

1961, the other three leading indicators reached their peaks before the 500 stock average, thus predicting the coming stock peaks.

Business Conditions Digest is available from the Government Printing Office, Washington, D.C., at $16 per year.

One thing you have to count on in any economic planning is the surety of future inflation. In 1969 I wrote a book called *How You Can Beat Inflation*. When many politicians claimed that inflation was licked, and when a great many economists agreed with them, I predicted that for years to come inflation would continue as a bogey—that it would worsen and would prove unbeatable no matter how strenuous the efforts to contain it. Forces at work in a welfare state are too strong. Inflation, I wrote, has acquired a life of its own.

Although scoffed at by economists, this view has proved to be correct. Inflation now has a life of its own. It feeds on too-great money supply increases by the Federal Reserve, on union contracts and management greed, and on the desire of citizens for more governmental goodies than can be furnished on the kind of balanced budget that can contain inflation.

My prediction now: Expect more—and worse—inflation ahead.

One thing inflation will bring about is a shortage of corporate capital and of funds to lend. There will be no more of the easy 2 and 3 and 4 percent interest rates of the fifties. The reason is simple: A lender can count, say, upon 6 percent inflation. When he recognizes that 6 percent of the real value of money he lends out is going to be gobbled away by insidious inflation, he knows that to get a *true* 2 percent yield, he has to charge the borrower a big 8 percent interest. It is a tough bit of reasoning, but accurate.

There is a borrower advantage in this prospect of endless inflation, though. Say you borrow $10,000 for one year (we'll use a single year to make this example simple). You, like the lender, know about inevitable inflation. Like the lender, you figure—probably with accuracy—on 6 percent. *That means that if you borrow $10,000, you'll only have to pay back $9,400 in real dollars of the purchasing power of the dollars you borrow.* So if you have to pay 8 percent, but gain 6 percent in shrinkage of the amount you must repay, you will shell out only a true 2 percent in interest. It's not so bad when looked at in that light.

That is the only realistic light in which to look at things since inflation will be with us for many years to come. If it changes, it will get worse rather than better. Don't believe soothing sayings or the pontifications of academic economists when they tell you otherwise. Remember that the statement about worsening inflation is made by a man who said it before, was scoffed at—and was proved right.

How did this horrible problem come about?

Inflation means that more and more money chases the same goods, a trend that began in the late sixties when the Federal Reserve expanded money supply at a frighteningly fast rate. The average rate of increase during post-World War II years was about 2.5 percent. This kept pace with the increase in productivity. The swollen 6 percent money stock increases of the Johnson and Nixon administrations, though, were far in excess of increases in productivity.

The Federal Reserve in 1969 stopped money supply growth. Predictably, the economy began to turn over like a dying whale as recession took hold. Alarmed, the Federal Reserve in early 1970—while still talking monetary restraint—began to inflate the money supply even more. From February 1970 to June 1970, money supply increased at a 9.8 percent (annual) rate of growth.

Meanwhile, prices tended to increase even faster than they had before because of a second cause of inflation—cost-push inflation.

Consider what wage increases mean. A manufacturer's costs go up. So he raises the price by a small percentage and ships his merchandise to the wholesaler. The truck line that carries the goods must pay higher wages. It, too, raises the tab for carrying the goods to the distributor.

In order not to be swamped under the increases, the wholesaler is forced to add a normal mark-up to the increases themselves. (Sometimes, if he is greedy, he chews off a bit of extra increase while he is about it.) Then he ships to the retail store. Again, the merchandise moves in union-manned trucks, and again the cost of transportation is higher, so that there is a series of increases on the cost by the time this merchandise reaches the retailer. He, too, is compelled to add his regular mark-up percentage to the increases themselves as well as to the old base price, and he may add a further increase he is not compelled to have. Now, when the merchandise reaches the consumer, the percentage is no longer small. The price has been upped a great deal.

Now that we have seen the effects of the two major causes of inflation, we still must consider how these causes come into being. First, how does the money supply expand? One way is called "open market operations."

The Federal Reserve has to expand and contract money stock all the time. This is necessary because of such factors as seasonal business needs. All works well unless productivity gains are not as large as money supply inflation. Assume the Fed feels a $10 billion injection of money is in order. The system's Open Market Committee enters an order to purchase $10 billion in Treasury Bonds from a dealer we'll call Bill Bondseller. To pay for the purchase, the Fed credits Bill's bank $10 billion, which the banker then credits to the Bondseller. Suddenly $10 billion, nonexistent before this transaction, has entered the economy.

Or the Fed might decide to change bank reserves. Say the Eighth National has $5 billion in deposits but must maintain 20 percent reserves ($1 billion). If the Federal Reserve

changes that to 15 percent, the bank can begin to lend out
$250 million it could not have dispensed before. Those dol-
lars become, in effect, an addition to working money.

Now for the second cause of inflation. How did cost-push
get underway in the first place? The Federal Reserve Bank of
Philadelphia had this to say in a study on inflation ("Henry
VIII Revisited"), which was reported in its *Business Review*:

> The cost-push theory of inflation rests on the premise that
> fundamental changes have taken place in our economy during
> the twentieth century. The theory points out that business firms
> have expanded in size and influence. Labor unions have grown
> in strength and bargaining power. Indeed, according to the cost-
> push thesis, labor today is so powerful at the bargaining table
> that it can push up wages faster than productivity (output per
> man-hour). Consequently, costs per unit of output increase.
> And rising costs are a source of great concern to management.
>
> As costs rise, management has two choices. It can absorb the
> increased cost and thus experience falling profit margins; or it
> can pass costs on to the consumer in the form of higher prices
> if in a market position to do so. Since business has grown in
> influence and market power, there is a tendency to choose the
> latter alternative—to raise prices rather than lose profits.
>
> But what does this have to do with money? . . . Plenty, say the
> cost-push theorists.
>
> In 1946, Congress passed a law—the Employment Act of
> 1946—which, among other things, calls upon the federal
> government to help maintain maximum employment. To
> achieve this objective, it is necessary for virtually all goods pro-
> duced to be purchased, even at higher price levels generated by
> cost-push pressures. If some goods are not bought, business
> will lay off workers. There will be unemployment.
>
> But where will we get the additional money to purchase the
> same amount of goods at higher price? Not every salary of every
> worker will be raised. . . . There is a limit to the extent people
> will spend their hard-earned savings and part with cash. At this
> point they will decrease their consumption. Then, conclude the
> cost-push theorists, the federal government is forced to step in.
> To maintain employment, the state must take steps to increase

the amount of money available for spending. In short, it would be forced to manufacture money.

What will all this mean by, say, 1979? I have in front of me a Bureau of Labor Statistics release, which shows that from January 1967 to January 1969 the consumer price index for urban wage earners rose from 114.7 to 124.1. Ten years before, using the same months (January 1957 compared to January 1959), the rise was from 99.7 to 102.2. In two years during the fifties, inflation, measured by the BLS Consumer Price Index, went up by 4.8 percent. *But in two comparable years in the sixties, it went up 8.25 percent.*

Say that the rate doubles in ten years, as it did in the last decade, and the rate of every two-years' increase will stay at 8.2 percent for the next four years. For the four years that follow, it will be at 1.5 times that rate (12.3 percent), and for the final two-year period it will be double the 1967-1969 rate.

That would raise the Consumer Price Index to a lofty 213.4.

At that level, the dollar would have depreciated in purchasing power by a further 72 percent.

In my earlier book, *How You Can Beat Inflation*, I pointed out that, given such an increase (which I believe is probably on the low side), "the medium-sized car . . . in the area of $4,000, would then cost $6,880. The $50 supermarket checkout ticket of today would have run up to $86 without your having purchased a single additional item. The $35,000 house of today would be up in the area of $60,200 and not have a single air conditioner, kitchen fixture, or carpet added to it. If you now paid $200 a month to buy this house, ten years hence you would be writing a check in the amount of $344. . . . You would be in what today are considered upper income cost brackets without necessarily having achieved upper income frills."

Why isn't something being done about this? Because it is politically unpalatable to take truly effective steps to stop inflation.

We're a welfare state in which all groups of people, from Social Security pensioners to corporate executives, depend to an increasing degree upon the government to hand them the goodies of life. We call upon the government whenever we have a problem. Do hospital stays cost a lot? We invent Medicare. Do pensioners have trouble getting by? We increase Social Security payouts, without regard to the imbalance between amounts the recipients have paid and the sums they extract from the fund. We do this in a thousand ways. While all this rolls its merry way, the Department of Defense pushes government costs still higher.

During the years since we supposedly made ourselves secure by downing Germany and Japan, the federal government has made its people very insecure by having a balanced budget in only three of the years since "peace" came in 1945.

An unbalanced budget seems an unimportant thing to most people. And so it is if it occurs seldom enough. In our happy land, it occurs anything but seldom.

It wouldn't matter greatly if your family or business were to run a deficit year once or twice. If you or your business ran a deficit as the U.S. does, just about every time out, you'd be broke. The government is not broke because it has the happy ability (for politicians, not citizens) to run deficits all the time by manufacturing money. This it does. Thus inflation.

Our leaders give forth words about austerity and fighting inflation and living within our means. But when it really comes to living within our means or facing austerity, we turn away. It is not politically palatable. So our politicians, with the next elections ever before their eyes, turn again to the easy step of money manufacture. The dragon grows fat thereby.

Will wage and price controls stop this process? Consider the words of Darryl R. Francis, president of the Federal Reserve Bank of St. Louis. Recently, Mr. Francis noted that "Direct controls, like a new paint job over a termite-infested house, hide the evidence but do nothing to eliminate the cause."

Wage and price controls are not entirely without effect, however. They have, in fact, always brought on two effects. The imposition of these controls can probably be counted upon to produce the same effects again, and if you are to survive profitably, you have to know what they are and plan to meet them.

The first effect of price-wage controls is usually scarcity. When a product cannot be produced profitably, its maker switches his production to other products, which he hopes will not be controlled as closely or possibly will escape controls.

No manufacturer can continue production at a loss and stay in business; nor is he likely to continue with a tiny profit when by changing to another area he can switch back to the profit path.

Scarcities are likely to develop in labor, too. Workers have alternatives to working at controlled wages: unemployment insurance and, in many cases, welfare. In some areas, a large family on welfare can receive an income that almost reaches five figures. Rather than work for a wage no higher than this, some workers will opt for welfare. Not a pretty thought, but one with whose effects you must reckon.

Faced with such inflationary pushes and the need to gauge the economic climate accurately, it is important to know where you can turn for business and monetary counseling. Don't believe that counsel is always—even a majority of times—correct; judge it by the light of what we've seen earlier in this chapter. *But listen to it.* Advice is something to be heard and considered rather than blindly followed.

An army of experts is now deployed. They won't come to your assistance unasked, however. You first must locate them and next know how to retain them.

Mass Counseling

Long ago, psychologists discovered the merits (and money-saving features) of mass counseling by putting patients together and guiding them to help each other find solutions. Much the same technique is working in solving specialized operational problems. It can work in your city, too, given proper organization, which you might spearhead.

In an advisory put out by the U.S. Small Business Administration, *Mass Counseling Clinics for Small Business Managers*, James E. Estes, then Coordinator of Management Education Programs at the College of Business Administration of the University of Arkansas, wrote that

> findings of this experiment indicate that clinics for mass counseling can be quite successful. It was also found, however, that certain conditions have an impact on the degree of success.
>
> An important factor in the mass counseling clinics studied was that participating companies in each clinic were all engaged in the same type of work.
>
> The information must be detailed and specifically adapted to the companies participating. It should be limited to a narrow range of subject matter so that when the managers return to their companies they can concentrate their efforts on one set of changes.
>
> One day of intensive presentation of highly technical information can provide the typical small business manager with the optimum amount of information to be absorbed, retained, and applied in his company.
>
> The clinic or conference leader must be an expert in his subject area. He must also have many years of work experience in the specific segment of the industry represented at the clinic.
>
> If possible, one or more trade associations should participate in the clinics. The associations can help to (1) determine the subject matter most needed; (2) work out the details of presenting the clinic; and (3) motivate managers to attend.

Professional Business Consultants

"You have to remember this about the consultants," warned a man who had recently gone into business, partly on the advice of such a consultant. "Some of these guys are good—but expensive. Some of them are just expensive. I worked with two firms. One of these charged heavily to tell me that the area in which I was interested was on the west bank of the Mississippi River—the naked eye told that—and to give me some complicated population trend figures that anyone could obtain over the telephone from a research assistant at the public library. This firm suggested I interview similar businesses in several cities. Then it charged me for feeding back my own interview material.

"I hit finally upon a really good firm," my friend continued, "after I had talked to many people and investigated the reputation and financial standing of each outfit. Such investigation is better than just consulting the firm with a first telephone directory listing."

Trade-Professional Societies

Sometimes the principal purpose of these societies consists in what is politely called education of legislators—in other words, lobbying. With or without such outside "educational" activities, most trade associations and professional groups spread a great deal of information among their members.

"I was amazed," one businessman said recently, "to find out that the help I had thought hard to obtain was readily available in existing presentations of the society to which I belong. In addition, since I'm in the area of association headquarters, they sent out an expert to survey my particular problems."

Play It as a Game

The computer has made possible all kinds of simulation, in which projections are played out against a background of known conditions. Describing one such "game" at the Bureau of Business Research, University of Texas, a Management Research Summary of the Small Business Administration reported:

During the past several years, management-decision simulation has become increasingly popular as a training device. In these business games, the players receive detailed information about a simulated firm and its economic environment. The players, as executives of the fictional company, make a series of business decisions, which are fed into an electronic data processing computer.

The computer then produces reports showing the effect of the decisions on the business, and players use these reports as the basis for further decisions. The players are thus able to simulate several years of decision making—and to see the results of their decisions. . . . In the game discussed here, the situations in which the players find their firms at the beginning are such that successful corporate performances are not possible within the framework of the "existing" conditions. Solutions to the environmental problem can be worked out, however, by means of new product development and new geographic market penetration.

A key feature of the simulation is that the moves that can be made are not initially revealed to the participants. The players are told that they may ask the administrator of the game for information not included in initial briefing papers or in the periodic reports from the computer. They are also advised that they may propose changes in their method of operation.

This open-end feature of the game has proved most successful. Psychologically, it leads participants to identify themselves very closely with their simulated enterprises. More important, it permits the administrator to encourage players to (1) recognize the barriers to company growth, (2) seek information regarding possible solutions, and (3) propose and carry out "escape" solutions. . . . Experience with these sessions suggests that the simulation can be used successfully in small-business management courses and executive-development programs. Its two outstanding advantages are: (1) the possibility of integrating the activity with other demands on the participants' time, and (2) the high motivation and interest of participants in the problems generated by the simulation.

Such a problem-solving gambit need not depend upon the

computer, however. Reporting on a noncomputerized business game developed at the University of Houston, another SBA Research Summary noted:

> The report discussed in this Summary presents a low-cost, flexible business simulation game—MANTRAP Management Training Program—that does not require a computer. MANTRAP differs from computer simulations in that it emphasizes nonquantitative aspects of the decision maker's problem of obtaining and evaluating information under restrictions of time and money.
>
> The players are faced with situations requiring solutions but are not given all the information they need to develop a decision. They are left with the problem of deciding on the information needed, getting the information, and analyzing it. To play the game effectively, they must develop a strategy of securing the processing information. This involves problems of organization to reduce the time and cost needed for decisions.
>
> MANTRAP can be played almost anywhere by from 1 to 50 players. It can be played in one long, intensive day, two comfortably full days, or three long evenings, either on successive days or spread over a longer period. . . . The players, either as individuals or organized into teams of from two to seven members, enter the game as executive officers of a going concern. Each has been furnished, in the Player's Manual, with a history of the industry and of his own fictional firm, including its financial history up to the last six months. . . . After receiving the situation descriptions, the players are given from thirty to forty-five minutes to decide on a course of action. They may apply for information to the administrator of the game, who in a sense functions as a staff assistant. He indicates whether the information is available and how much it will cost. (A time factor may also be introduced.) Players must decide how much they can spend on information, keeping in mind that many pertinent internal reports are free.
>
> Reliable sources of information are presented in the form of reports from trade associations, technical journals, government agencies, market research agencies, consultants, internal research and development, social contacts, and business trips.

None of the information offered is wrong, but it may be misleading or irrelevant. Players cannot buy all the available information; and if they could, it would not, in most cases, be complete enough to determine a choice automatically.

The collection of items of information that may be "purchased" by the players in effect creates a business world. The players learn about this simulated business world by buying information or ideas from the information sources.

Tap the Oldtimers' Wisdom

In many areas, retired executives have banded together to act as consultants, sometimes unpaid, sometimes at moderate pay. Exploring this avenue can open up a mine of expertise not learned from books but from actual experience.

See the CPA

Larger firms of Certified Public Accountants are answering the demands of their clients for wider advice by opening full consulting departments. Your accounting firm may have such advisory talent on tap or might be able to suggest a colleague who offers the service.

Bank on Your Banker

Like the CPA, the banker is called upon to help in a wide variety of nonfinancial ways. A Chicago bank has nearly twenty specialized consulting and operational services.

Publications

Magazines of the field exist to receive and pass along ideas that have worked. "Go thou and do likewise" is the angle of nearly every article showing operational ideas of one firm that can be adapted to another.

Those Who Work for You

Employee suggestions are a fruitful source of ideas. "Why pay an expensive outside consultant who is perhaps familiar with the field in general but not usually with my particular problems, when strong likelihood exists that in my employee suggestion box there will be an idea that comes from someone equally familiar with the field and in addition versed in the workings of *this* firm?" one administrator asked.

3: The First Big Decisions

T HE first decision you must make after realizing that your projected new business will require outside money is whether you want to go the equity route or the debt route—or both.

Equity is defined by my desk dictionary as meaning "fairness, impartiality, justice . . . anything that is fair or equitable . . . the value of property beyond the total amount owed on it." Our area of interest lies in the third sense of the word.

Debt, on the other hand, the dictionary defines as "an obligation or liability to pay or return something . . . the condition of owing, as to be in debt . . . in theology, a sin." All except the last sense are appropriate here.

If you go the equity route in raising money for your new business (or getting additional capital for the existing business that can't be expanded without it but might go over big with extra money), then you'll be giving away part of the ownership of the business. Equity financing boils down to that. You either go public by selling stock, after first incorporating the

30

business, or else you take in a partner or partners who become owner(s) of varying amounts and percentages of the operation.

Thus, when you finance through equity you sell a part of the ownership. It is irrevocable. You can't (unless the new owners agree) grab back that percentage you sold. It is theirs forever, or at any rate until the business liquidates or they decide to sell their share.

An advantage of equity financing—if feasible in the circumstances—is that you don't have to repay it, or even shell out a dividend or partnership share if the majority ownership decides that such money might better be plowed back into the business for expansion. The disadvantage, obviously, is that what was once yours in full is yours in complete ownership no longer. You have to take into account the interests, needs, and desires of other people who, whether you like the idea or not, are forever part owners.

If you go the debt route, on the other hand, you borrow money. You might do it through a bank loan or some other type of direct loan, including money lent by rich Uncle Teddy, whose only heir and present pride and joy you are. Debt financing includes sale of bonds, secured or otherwise (*debentures* are unsecured bonds), and loans from any of the sources mentioned in chapter one.

An advantage of debt financing is that you don't have to please, coddle, or otherwise give a hoot about other owners. (If you're in default on the debt later on, this doesn't apply; creditors can and often do take over management of a company, entirely legally, in order to effect measures which are deemed wise in recovering amounts lent and interest owed by a defaulting debtor.) A disadvantage is that the interest payments, as well as the principal payments necessary to retire the debt, are to be met—if not forever, at least for that part of eternity during which the debt runs.

However, the fact of debt offers a tax advantage. Meeting interest obligations on a debt is an expense of doing business and is counted in computing net income. Thus it comes off the top *before* taxes and, depending upon the tax bracket in which you find yourself as the new business expands and succeeds, the Bureau of Internal Revenue meets a part of the cost of interest. Not so dividends paid to stockholders. These come *after* computation of net income. You can't consider them a business expense—they are a reward to stockholders for backing a successful venture—and they are emphatically *not* a tax deductible item.

These are simplified definitions of the initial big choice that must be made. Now let's look at the matter in greater detail. The following discussion is from a "Going Public Workshop" sponsored by the University of Arizona:

> We are often asked to evaluate certain factors that are normally considered in deciding whether to remain private, go public, be acquired, or seek other alternatives. The purpose of this memorandum is to outline certain of the factors that are normally considered in making this evaluation.
>
> As a practical matter, the factors and problems that should be considered by a firm in one industry or with one type of product may be far different from those that need to be considered by a firm in another industry or with another type of product. For example, special problems need to be considered for service businesses, such as how stockholders/employees will be motivated and how rewards will be related to performance after a public offering. This has been a special problem for certain service companies that have gone public, e.g., advertising agencies.
>
> In addition, there are many other characteristics of a business that may have a bearing upon the evaluation, e.g., the goals and objectives of the company and its stockholders, its age or maturity, its financing needs, competition, etc. These characteristics usually have a great effect upon the evaluation of each alternative. They should be considered and discussed in depth.
>
> Finally, private-company stockholders should be aware of the fact that what is personally pleasing to them in the short-term may not be in the long-term.

The private firm has the following alternatives available to finance its growth and/or transfer ownership:

1. Remain private; finance expansion with retained earnings, debt and collateral arrangements such as lease financing, joint ventures, marketing/distribution agreements, licensing agreements, etc.; transfer ownership by death, gift, buy-sell agreements, etc.
2. Sell stock to the public; use the funds received for expansion or other purposes.
3. Merge with or be acquired by a public company.
4. Sell stock to a minority investor(s) in a private placement; use the funds received for expansion or other purposes.

Following is a discussion outline of certain of the factors that are generally considered by private companies and/or their stockholders in evaluating the above alternatives.

Remain Private

There are many possible advantages to remaining private that are often overlooked. In addition, private stockholders often do not have an awareness or an understanding of the capital that is available to their firm. They may not realize that lease financing, borrowing from company pension funds, factoring or commercial and installment financing, Small Business Administration financing, financing available from wealthy private individuals through the use of tax shelters, cash value life insurance loans, and a variety of other means may satisfy their long-term financing needs, in addition, of course, to the more conventional financing which may be available from banks, insurance companies, and others. Where such alternatives exist, it may not be beneficial to give up private status.

Some of the factors that are normally considered in deciding whether or not to remain private are the following:

1. *Control*
   a. Some loss of control when private status is abandoned, which is often repugnant to stockholders.
   b. Possible consequences of loss of control include forced retirement, loss of employment for family members, basic conflict of goals and objectives, surrender of major decisions to others.

2. *Continuity of Management*
   a. Difficult problem in private firm since the trend is away from "following in father's footsteps."
   b. Factors which contribute to the problem include: Other members in family may lack interest in the business or lack professional skills; executive incentives, e.g., stock options, are often unavailable.
   c. In the large, professionally managed private firm, this may not be a major problem, providing adequate executive incentives exist.
   d. Possible solutions without surrendering private-firm status include gradual sale of business to the next generation of management (buy-sell agreements) or other classes of employees (Kelso or Second Income Plans).
3. *Personal Characteristics of the Business*
   a. The private firm can maintain secrecy of operations, financial conditions, ownership, etc., and also avoid publicity.
   b. The stockholders have substantial freedom in dealing with the firm; benefits include quasi-personal expenses and loans from the business and determination of own duties and responsibilities.
   c. Value of the private business generally depends mainly on the performance of management—distribution of rewards (profits) and ultimate redemption of ownership interests is normally not based on the stock market or other external variables but on the actual earnings and net worth of the business.
4. *Future Potential*
   The private firm may lack certain essential ingredients for sustained growth, e.g., marketing-distribution or technical skills or financial resources; if another alternative would supply these ingredients, the rewards to the stockholders could thereby be increased.
5. *Estate and Investment Planning*
   a. Private status may or may not result in the greatest estate tax savings for the owners in the area of valuation and excess accumulated earnings tax problems; it may

make it difficult for an executor to sell the company's stock to pay taxes, debts and bequests.

    b. Private status may not be consistent with the stock-holders' investment planning, i.e., greater diversification and marketability of the stockholders' investment might be achieved through cash sale to a larger firm or exchange for its marketable securities. Such greater diversification and liquidity of investment can result in lower risk for the stockholders.

6. *Cost of Doing Business*
    a. Accounting, legal, printing, public/stockholder relations, and administrative costs are usually lower.
    b. Financing costs may be high.
    c. Other costs may be higher if the firm is small due to diseconomies of scale.

7. *Availability of Expansion Capital*
    a. May be limited for private firm.
    b. Solution—there may still be many ways of obtaining required financing, e.g., lease and installment financing, borrowing from company pension funds, employee stock purchase plans, SBA financing, financing from the personal wealth and credit of the owners and/or friends, cash surrender value insurance loans, etc.

8. *Other*

The corporate image of the private firm and interest in it by customers, suppliers, employees, and others may not be as great as it could be were the firm publicly owned or a subsidiary of a public firm.

Sell Stock to the Public

The following is a summary of the advantages and disadvantages of going public:

1. *Cost*
    a. Legal, accounting, printing, underwriting, filing, and other similar nonrecurring costs are high.
    b. Certain continuing costs of a public firm are also high relative to the private firm, e.g., public/stockholder rela-

tions, reporting requirements, legal, accounting, printing, etc.
c. Considerable time is required to complete an offering.
d. Future financing costs are normally reduced if the offering is successful.
e. Future availability of capital is normally greater but it is
not assured—stock price or performance may deterior-
ate; small "float" may inhibit future financing.
2. *Control*
a. Some loss of control occurs—new "owners," directors,
etc.
b. Undesirability of this loss of control depends upon the
personalities, adaptability, and personal desires of the
owners.
3. *Continuity of Management*
a. May improve the ability of the firm to attract professional managers (through stock options, higher salaries,
etc.) and "outside" directors who often can provide
valuable assistance.
b. In some cases, however, it may make it more difficult to
attract professional managers since the rewards may be
less after offering (as in some service businesses).
c. Size of firm, potential, and type of product, service, or
industry are as important in judging the ability of the
firm to attract professional managers.
4. *Personal Characteristics of the Business*
a. Many are sacrificed, e.g., quasi-personal expenses and
employee/stockholder loans; secrecy of operations,
ownership, etc.; lack of publicity; freedom of operation;
lack of restrictions.
b. The stockholders may find the immediate and near
complete loss of privacy difficult to adjust to.
5. *Estate and Investment Planning*
a. May help solve some estate tax problems in the area of
valuation and excess accumulated earnings tax; however,
it often does not solve estate and investment planning
problems; a small "float" may make subsequent sale of
significant amounts of stock by the control stockholders
difficult and may inhibit the ease of valuation—small

"float" requires that control stockholders sell very small amounts of stock over a long period of time; this reduces marketability and possibly proceeds from sales.
   b. May improve investment—marketability, liquidity.
6. *Acquisitions*
Acquisitions of or mergers with other firms are often easier when public security exists; securities of a private firm are usually unacceptable to stockholders of another firm. However, going public makes subsequent acquisition by another company more difficult.
7. *Other*
   a. May not solve anything if a firm's basic problem is lack of marketing, production, technical, or other skills.
   b. May improve the corporate image of the business and the interest in it by customers, suppliers, employees, and others; this may improve its marketing capability.
   c. Rewards to stockholders depend upon many other factors besides the performance of the management and the earnings and net worth of the business—stock market, industry developments, broker recommendations, etc.

Merger with or Acquisition by a Public Company
The alternative of merging with, or being acquired by, another firm has become popular among private companies in the past decade. Tight financial markets, increased competition in most industries, willingness of many corporations to make acquisitions at high prices, and other factors have influenced private firms to seek affiliation with other larger firms.

APB Opinion Numbers 16 and 17 specify certain accounting practices to be followed in accounting for mergers and acquisitions. Opinion 16 provides specific criteria as to whether a business combination is to be accounted for as a purchase or a pooling of interests. Combinations which meet the pooling criteria must be accounted for as pooling and all others as purchases. Opinion 17 requires that any goodwill arising in business combinations accounted for as purchases be amortized over a period not to exceed forty years. These opinions can have a significant impact on the private firm's evaluation of the merger/acquisition alternative. For example, if earnings are high in relation to book value, as in many service businesses, a pooling transaction may be necessary because of the substantial goodwill and amortization that would normally result in a business combination accounted for as a purchase. In this case, the payment of cash and/or consideration based upon a future earnings or market action contingency (after consummation of the transaction) is generally prohibited. Thus the private stockholders may be forced to accept stock, or, if they insist upon cash and/or a contingency arrangement, they may have to settle for a substantially reduced price for their business.

Some of the factors that are normally considered before deciding whether or not to be acquired are the following:

1. *Control*
   a. Usually there is substantial loss of control, although a great deal of operating freedom may be retained.
   b. Pressure for survival on former stockholders may be reduced when control passes.
2. *Continuity of Management*
   This problem is usually solved when sale is effected.
3. *Personal Characteristics of the Business*
   Loss of personal characteristics is usually not as great as in a public offering; quasi-personal expenses and freedom of operation are usually lost to some degree, but some privacy may be retained.
4. *Estate and Investment Planning*
   a. If the stock received is readily marketable, this route usually solves many of the stockholders' estate and investment planning problems—liquidity, marketability, diversification, valuation, excess accumulated earnings tax problems—although this depends upon the acquiring company's size, nature of its business, and distribution of its stock.
   b. Future value of the investment depends upon the performance of the combined business rather than the individual performance of the acquired firm; efforts of the acquired firm may not affect the value of the investment as directly—could be good or bad.
   c. Significant loss in value of investment is possible in a

stock transaction if the securities received are overpriced or if there is a subsequent general decline in the stock market.

5. *Addition of Required Assets or Skills*

Most compelling reason to seek sale or merger—add necessary ingredients for sustained growth, e.g., financial resources, additional customers, new skills, research and development capability, etc.

6. *Cost of Doing Business*
   a. Certain costs do increase once a firm becomes a division or subsidiary of another company, e.g., reporting and accounting costs, budgetary and planning costs, etc.
   b. Other costs may be reduced substantially, e.g., financing, production (due to increased volume), research and development, bookkeeping (if centralized computer is used).

Sell Stock to a Minority Investor(s) in a Private Placement

Private placement as an alternative for the private firm has grown in popularity in the past decade. Venture capital investing has long been a favorite pastime of wealthy individuals and families. Stories of high returns on investment by these individuals and families encouraged the growth of institutionalized venture capital firms, initially Small Business Investment Companies (SBIC's), then venture capital partnerships, public venture funds, and corporate venture capital pools.

APB Opinion Number 18 has also contributed to the recent popularity of private placement/minority investment. Under APB Opinion Number 18, a minority investor who owns 20 percent or more of the voting securities of another company can normally report its share of the earnings of the investee; consequently, minority investment can be used by mature firms to provide young businesses with needed assets and skills without sacrifice of control by the investee and without dilution of earnings for the investor. Subsequent sale of the minority investment is often easier for the same reasons.

The following factors are generally considered in deciding whether or not to effect a private placement:

1. *Cost*
    a. Small in relation to public offering—time and reports required are minimal.
    b. Cost of capital may be greater than conventional types of financing or a public offering—investor expects impressive gains for risk taken.
    c. Cost of capital may be less because of other financing available after the private placement, e.g., capital made available by insurance companies, banks, and others because of their contact with the investor.
2. *Control*
    a. Some loss of control—less than sale or merger but often more than a public offering.
    b. Investor normally selects one or more representatives on the board, restricts decisions on purchase or sale of assets, controls future financing and issuance of stock and debt instruments, can replace specified officers in certain circumstances.
    c. Basic conflicts in personalities, goals, and objectives can result; investor may want to sell his investment in 3-5 years which may be unacceptable to the stockholders or inconsistent with the long-term plans of the firm.
3. *Continuity of Management*
    a. Private investor can help solve this problem—the additional financing may make attractive executive compensation programs possible; the investor's contact with experienced, professional managers can make it easier to provide continuity.
    b. One of the most popular attractions, stock options, is still generally not available, although it may be promised if a public offering is planned.
4. *Personal Characteristics of the Business*
    Stockholders retain most of the personal characteristics of their business; however, they must normally separate quasi-personal expenses from the firm.
5. *Estate and Investment Planning*
    a. Private placement does not directly help this planning, although it could help provide an indication of value for estate tax purposes.

    b. May build a "bridge" to a public offering or sale which would help.
6. *Addition of Needed Assets and Skills*
    a. Most compelling reason to select private placement—can provide skills and access to financial resources, contacts, and sponsorship lacking in a young firm until it develops greater maturity.
    b. Unless private investor does provide this, it is often a very expensive type of financing.
7. *Other*
  Minority investment can be used by two firms to learn more about each other prior to a possible merger.

In the preceding chapter we examined how to determine the most favorable business climate for financing a new business. We have now looked at the avenues and early decisions.

Whoever does the financing will have to make some decisions, too. He will have to determine something about you and the probability that you can (or can't) make a go of the new venture. This is a subjective decision; only the future can tell him factually, but he will size you up, perhaps ask for certain financial data, and certainly run exhaustive examinations of your past.

Other decisions are objective—or nearly so. They can be based upon facts. Whether he is looking at you as a borrower, a possible stockholder, or a venture into which to place private capital, you'll have to be prepared with certain financial statements. They should be as factual as possible. Cheat and you'll get caught, sacrifice your chance of a lifetime, and maybe find that you have overstepped a legal line as well.

Some ventures, being new, can't furnish profit and loss statements or balance sheets. *Do a projected one.* Do it as exhaustively as you can. Gather data on what might happen under varying conditions, and from these figures and expected events extrapolate the statements that will be required.

If possible, go to a Certified Public Accountant for help. If he throws up his hands and says that the task is impossible, don't be discouraged. Go to other firms. Eventually you will find—possibly among the big outfits that have dealt with financing in the past—an understanding of your needs. From your raw figures, ask the CPA to assemble statements. He will mark these with a statement like this: "Prepared from furnished figures." That indicates that he's merely done the assembling and is in no way certifying the factuality of what you have offered.

An expert, Verne A. Bunn, can help you assemble. In a Small Business Administration booklet titled *Buying and Selling a Small Business*, Mr. Bunn noted:

> The first and most logical step is to conduct a market analysis. A market analysis is a study of the present position of the business within its market area and of probably future patterns. It should include the growth pattern of the business, . . . the state of the market, the nature and extent of competition—all factors, in fact, that will show the present market position of the business or that will affect its future. . . .
>
> The specific nature of the business . . . will determine much of the market information needed. A manufacturing business with problems of marketing and distribution will need information not necessarily pertinent to a retail or service business, with its more localized market. The following areas of market information are designed to suggest sources that may be useful to the buyer or the seller in analyzing the market of the business. . . .
>
> A study of the cost of goods sold is also important in determining the market position of the business. Cost of goods sold is the cost of merchandise purchased by the business for resale, including freight and other charges. The difference between sales and the cost of the goods sold is called *gross margin* or *gross profit*. The higher the cost of goods sold in relation to sales, the lower the gross margin—and the net profit.
>
> Many factors, both within the company and in the market of which the business is a part, affect the cost of goods sold. An investigation should be made to determine the following:

1. *Average rate of stock turnover* . . . for similar businesses.

2. *Extent to which invoices are being discounted.* Paying invoices in time to earn the cash discount will increase both gross margin and net profit if the discount is recorded as a reduction in the cost of goods sold. A direct increase in net profit will result if the discount is shown as "other income."

3. *Freight costs* . . .

Unless the business has a monopoly of some sort, a study of the competition should be included in the market analysis. The competition may be local and well defined, or quite generalized, depending on the nature of the business and of the market.

Trade associations and other data-gathering agencies, both governmental and nongovernmental, are sometimes helpful in this area. A good deal of the information about competition, however, must come from direct investigation, business by business.

Such factors as these are of interest: estimated sales, advertising and promotion, services offered, performance of sales personnel, businesses entering and leaving the competition recently, changes in the competitive structure through product mix or services offered, pricing policies, and other factors that form a part of the competitive patterns for specific types of businesses. A very important aspect of competition is the extent to which the total weight of competition has expanded the market for certain types of products or kinds of businesses, and the direction this is taking.

In certain businesses, location may not be too important, providing the physical plant is structurally sound and suitable for the business. In other cases, location may be a vital factor. An important point that should be looked into is the status of the location and any plans for proposed changes that may have an adverse effect on the future of the business. Urban renewal programs are causing many small businesses to look for new locations. So are changes in highways and streets, flood-control programs, changes in zoning ordinances and the like. . . .

The number of people within the market area and the amount of spendable income they have are important market factors. For many kinds of businesses, the total population is less important than certain segments of the population. A business selling hearing aids, for example, will be interested only in persons who have hearing difficulties.

In gathering information on income and expenditures, three factors should be kept in mind: (1) the total purchasing power based on total population; (2) the average or median income for the typical family unit; (3) the amount or percent of expenditure for various types of goods and services.

General population figures are obtained from federal, state, and local government sources. The federal census, taken every ten years, gives not only total population figures but also breakdowns that are useful in many business situations. For most of the larger cities, census figures are further classified by sections within the city on the basis of certain population and economic characteristics. These sections are called census tracts.

Business population figures may be available from numerous sources. The Yellow Pages of the telephone directory and the city directory are local sources that are immediately available. Chambers of commerce, trade associations, and state and federal government agencies can often be helpful.

The ten-year census reports the income for 20 percent of the total population on a national, state, county, city, and census-tract basis. Other information issued by the Department of Commerce can also be useful.

Many trade associations report the results of research on consumer expenditures. Other sources of data on income include the following: (1) planning commission offices, (2) employment offices, (3) research done by newspapers, (4) building permits, especially in newly developed areas, and (5) mortgage and loan companies. Numerous fact-gathering agencies develop and publish estimates of consumer income and expenditures for various classes of goods and services.

4: Borrowing from a Bank (and Other Lenders)

You have decided to go the debt route. You want to borrow the money needed to start that new business or expand the older one, which needs only a transfusion money to blossom into the big time—or nearly big time.

Where do you go? Whom do you see? What do you say him? How much will he lend you? On what terms?

Will you have to leave your grandmother in hock, along with the family's heirloom jewelry, all your stocks, and the future of your planned business?

In short, how do you go about borrowing?

That is the subject of this chapter. As always, let's have the experts tell it. In this case they are the Staff on Financ Assistance, Small Business Administration, Washington, D. In an advisory titled "The ABC's of Borrowing," they note

Inexperience with borrowing procedures often creat resentment and bitterness. The stories of three small busine men illustrate this point.

45

"I'll never trade here again," Bill Smith said when his bank refused to grant him a loan. "I'd like to let you have it, Bill," the banker said, "but your firm isn't earning enough to meet your current obligations." Mr. Smith was unaware of a vital financial fact, namely, that lending institutions have to be certain that the borrower's business can repay the loan.

Tom Jones lost his temper when the bank refused him a loan because he did not know what kind or how much money he needed. "We hesitate to lend," the banker said, "to businessmen with such vague ideas of what and how much they need."

John Williams's case was somewhat different. He didn't explode until after he got the loan. When the papers were ready to sign, he realized that the loan agreement put certain limitations on his business activities. "You can't dictate to me," he said and walked out of the bank. What he didn't realize was that the limitations were for his good as well as for the bank's protection.

Knowledge of the financial facts of life could have saved all three men the embarrassment of losing their tempers. Even more important, such information would have helped them to borrow money at a time when their businesses needed it badly. . . .

The ability to obtain money when you need it is as necessary to the operation of your business as is a good location or the right equipment, reliable sources of supplies and materials, or an adequate labor force. Before a bank or any other lending agency will lend you money, the loaning officer must feel satisfied with the answers to the five following questions:

1. What sort of person are you, the prospective borrower? By all odds, the character of the borrower comes first. Next is his ability to manage his business.

2. What are you going to do with the money? The answer to this question will determine the type of loan—short- or long-term. Money to be used for the purchase of seasonal inventory will require quicker repayment than money used to buy fixed assets.

3. When and how do you plan to pay it back? Your banker's judgment as to your business ability and the type of loan will be a deciding factor in the answer to this question.

4. Is the cushion in the loan large enough? In other words, does the amount requested make suitable allowance for unexpected developments? The banker decides this question on the basis of your financial statement, which sets forth the condition of your business, and/or on the collateral pledge.

5. What is the outlook for business in general and for your business particularly?

Adequate Financial Data Is a Must

The banker wants to make loans to businesses that are solvent, profitable, and growing. The two basic financial statements he uses to determine those conditions are the balance sheet and profit-and-loss statement. The former is the major yardstick for solvency and the latter for profits. A continuous series of these two statements over a period of time is the principal device for measuring financial stability and growth potential.

In interviewing loan applicants and in studying their records, the banker is especially interested in the following facts and figures.

General Information

Are the books and records up-to-date and in good condition? What is the condition of accounts payable? Of notes payable? What are the salaries of the owner-manager and other company officers? Are all taxes being paid currently? What is the order backlog? What is the number of employees? What is the insurance coverage?

Accounts Receivable

Are there indications that some of the accounts receivable have already been pledged to another creditor? What is the accounts receivable turnover? Is the accounts receivable total weakened because many customers are far behind in their payments? Has a large enough reserve been set up to cover doubtful accounts? How much do the largest accounts owe and what percentage of your total accounts does this amount represent?

Inventories

Is merchandise in good shape or will it have to be marked

down? How much raw material is on hand? How much work is in process? How much of the inventory is finished goods?

Is there any obsolete inventory? Has an excessive amount of inventory been consigned to customers? Is inventory turnover in line with the turnover for other businesses in the same industry? Or is money being tied up too long in inventory?

Fixed Assets

What is the type, age, and condition of the equipment? What are the depreciation policies? What are the details of mortgages or conditional sales contracts? What are the future acquisition plans?

Know Your Needs

When you set out to borrow money for your firm, it is important to know the kind of money you need from a bank or other lending institution. There are three kinds of money: short-term money, term money, and equity capital.

Keep in mind that the purposes for which the funds are to be used are an important factor in deciding the kind of money needed. But even so, deciding what kind of money to use is not always easy. It is sometimes complicated by the fact that you may be using some of various kinds of money at the same time and for identical purposes.

Keep in mind that a very important distinction between the types of money is the source of repayment. Generally, short-term loans are repaid from the liquidation of current assets which they have financed. Long-term loans are usually repaid from earnings.

Short-Term Bank Loans

You can use short-term bank loans for purposes such as financing accounts receivable for, say, thirty to sixty days. Or you can use them for purposes that take longer to pay off, such as for building a seasonal inventory over a period of five to six months. Usually, lenders expect short-term loans to be repaid after their purposes have been served; for example, accounts receivable loans, when the outstanding accounts have been paid by the borrower's customers, and inventory loans, when the inventory has been converted into saleable merchandise.

Banks grant such money either on your general credit reputation with an unsecured loan or on a secured loan—against collateral.

The *unsecured loan* is the most frequently used form of bank credit for short-term purposes. You do not have to put up collateral because the bank relies on your credit reputation.

The *secured loan* involves a pledge of some or all of your assets. The bank requires security as a protection for its depositors against the risks that are involved even in business situations where the chances of success are good.

Term Borrowing

Term borrowing provides money you plan to pay back over a fairly long time. Some people break it down into two forms: (1) intermediate—loans longer than one year but less than five years, and (2) long-term—loans for more than five years.

However, for your purpose of matching the kind of money to the needs of your company, think of term borrowing as a kind of money that you probably will pay back in periodic installments from earnings.

Equity Capital

Some people confuse term borrowing and equity (or investment) capital. Yet there is a big difference. You don't have to repay equity money. It is money you get by selling a part interest in your business.

You take people into your company who are willing to risk their money in it. They are interested in potential income rather than in an immediate return on their investment.

The amount of money you need to borrow depends on the purpose for which you need funds. Figuring the amount of money required for business construction, conversion, or expansion—term loans or equity capital—is relatively easy. Equipment manufacturers, architects, and builders will readily supply you with cost estimates. On the other hand, the amount of working capital you need depends upon the type of business you're in. While rule-of-thumb ratios may be helpful as a starting point, a detailed projection of sources and uses of funds over some future period of time—usually for twelve months—is a better approach. In this way, the characteristics of the particular situation can be taken into account. Such a projection is developed through the combination of a predicted budget and a cash forecast.

The budget is based on recent operating experience plus your best judgment of performance during the coming period. The cash forecast is your estimate of cash receipts and disbursements during the budget period. Thus, the budget and cash forecast together represent your plan for meeting your working capital requirements.

To plan your working capital requirements, it is important to know the "cash flow" that your business will generate. This involves simply a consideration of all elements of cash receipts and disbursements at the time they occur.

Sometimes, your signature is the only security the bank needs when making a loan. At other times, the bank requires additional assurance that the money will be repaid. The kind and amount of security depends on the bank and on the borrower's situation.

If the loan required cannot be justified by the borrower's financial statements alone, a pledge of security may bridge the gap. The types of security are: endorsers, co-makers, and guarantors; assignment of leases; warehouse receipts; trust receipts and floor planning; chattel mortgages; real estate; accounts receivable; savings accounts; life insurance policies; and stocks and bonds. In a substantial number of states where the Uniform Commercial Code has been enacted, paperwork for recording loan transactions will be greatly simplified.

Endorsers, Co-makers, and Guarantors

Borrowers often get other people to sign a note in order to bolster their own credit. These *endorsers* are contingently liable for the note they sign. If the borrower fails to pay up, the bank expects the endorser to make the note good. Sometimes, the endorser may be asked to pledge assets or securities that he owns.

A *co-maker* is one who creates an obligation jointly with the borrower. In such cases, the bank can collect directly from either the maker or the co-maker.

A *guarantor* is one who guarantees the payment of a note by signing a guaranty commitment. Both private and government lenders often require guarantees from officers of corporations in order to assure continuity of effective management. Sometimes, a manufacturer will act as guarantor for one of his customers.

Assignment of Leases

The assigned lease as security is similar to the guarantee. It is used, for example, in some franchise situations.

The bank lends money on a building and takes a mortgage. Then the lease, which the dealer and the parent franchise company work out, is assigned so that the bank automatically receives the rent payments. In this manner, the bank is guaranteed repayment of the loan.

Warehouse Receipts

Banks also take commodities as security by lending money on a warehouse receipt. Such a receipt is usually delivered directly to the bank and shows that the merchandise used as security either has been placed in a public warehouse or has been left on your premises under the control of one of your employees who is bonded (as in field warehousing). Such loans are generally made on staple or standard merchandise that can be readily marketed. The typical warehouse receipt loan is for a percentage of the estimated value of the goods as security.

Trust Receipts and Floor Planning

Merchandise such as automobiles, appliances, and boats has to be displayed to be sold. The only way many small marketers can afford such displays is by borrowing money. Such loans are often secured by a note and a trust receipt.

This trust receipt is the legal paper for floor planning. It is used for serial-numbered merchandise. When you sign one, you (1) acknowledge receipt of the merchandise, (2) agree to keep the merchandise in trust for the bank, and (3) promise to pay the bank as you sell the goods.

Chattel Mortgages

If you buy equipment such as a cash register or a delivery truck, you may want to get a chattel mortgage loan. You give the bank a lien on the equipment you are buying.

The bank also evaluates the present and future market value of the equipment being used to secure the loan. How rapidly will it depreciate? Does the borrower have the necessary fire, theft, property damage, and public liability insurance on the equipment? The banker has to be sure that the borrower protects the equipment.

Real Estate

Real estate is another form of collateral for long-term loans. When taking a real estate mortgage, the bank finds out: (1) the location of the real estate, (2) its physical condition, (3) its foreclosure value, and (4) the amount of insurance carried on the property.

Accounts Receivable

Many banks lend money on accounts receivable. In effect, you are counting on your customers to pay your note.

The bank may take accounts receivable on a *notification* or a *non-notification* plan. Under the notification plan, the purchaser of the goods is informed by the bank that his account has been assigned to it and he is asked to pay the bank. Under the non-notification plan, the borrower's customers continue to pay him the sums due on their accounts and he pays the bank.

Savings Accounts

Sometimes, you might get a loan by assigning to the bank a savings account. In such cases, the bank gets an assignment from you and keeps your passbook. If you assign an account in another bank as collateral, the lending bank asks the other bank to mark its records to show that the account is held as collateral.

Life Insurance

Another kind of collateral is life insurance. Banks will lend up to the cash value of a life insurance policy. You have to assign the policy to the bank.

If the policy is on the life of an executive of a small corporation, corporate resolutions must be made authorizing the assignment. Most insurance companies allow you to sign the policy back to the original beneficiary when the assignment to the bank ends.

Some people like to use life insurance as collateral rather than borrow directly from insurance companies. One reason is that a bank loan is often more convenient to obtain and usually may be obtained at a lower interest rate.

Stocks and Bonds

If you use stocks and bonds as collateral, they must be marketable. As a protection against market declines and possible expenses of liquidation, banks usually lend no more than 75 percent of the market value of high-grade stock. On federal government or municipal bonds, they may be willing to lend 90 percent or more of their market value.

The bank may ask the borrower for additional security or payment whenever the market value of the stocks or bonds drops below the bank's required margin.

Lending institutions are not just interested in loan repayments. They are also interested in borrowers with healthy profit-making businesses. Therefore, whether or not collateral is required for a loan, they set loan limitations and restrictions to protect themselves against unnecessary risk and at the same time against poor management practice by their borrowers. Often some owner-managers consider loan limitations a burden.

Yet others feel that such limitations also offer an opportunity for improving their management techniques.

Especially in making long-term loans, the borrower as well as the lender should be thinking of: (1) the net earning power of the borrowing company, (2) the capability of its management, (3) the long-range prospects of the company, and (4) the long-range prospects of the industry of which the company is a part. Such factors often mean that limitations increase as the duration of the loan increases.

The kinds of limitations that an owner-manager finds set

upon his company depend, to a great extent, on his company. If his company is a good risk, he should have only minimum limitations. A poor risk, of course, is different. Its limitations should be greater than those of a stronger company.

Look now for a few moments at the kinds of limitations and restrictions that the lender may set. Knowing what they are can help you see how they affect your operations.

The limitations that you will usually run into when you borrow money are: (1) repayment terms, (2) pledging or the use of security, and (3) periodic reporting.

A loan agreement, as you may already know, is a tailor-made document covering, or referring to, all the terms and conditions of the loan. With it, the lender does two things: (1) protects his position as a creditor (he wants to keep that position in as well-protected a state as it was on the date the loan was made) and (2) assures himself of repayment according to the terms.

The lender reasons that the borrower's business should generate enough funds to repay the loan while taking care of other needs. He considers that cash inflow should be great enough to do this without hurting the working capital of the borrower.

Covenants–Negative and Positive

The actual restrictions in a loan agreement come under a section known as covenants. Negative covenants are things that the borrower may not do without prior approval from the lender. Some examples are: further additions to the borrower's total debt, nonpledge to others of the borrower's assets, and issuance of dividends in excess of the terms of the loan agreement.

On the other hand, positive covenants spell out things that the borrower must do. Some examples are: (1) maintenance of a minimum net working capital, (2) carrying of adequate insurance, (3) repaying the loan according to the terms of the agreement, and (4) supplying the lender with financial statements and reports.

Overall, however, loan agreements may be amended from time to time and exceptions made. Certain provisions may be waived from one year to the next with the consent of the lender.

You Can Negotiate

Next time you go to borrow money, thresh out the lending terms before you sign. It is good practice no matter how badly you may need the money. Ask to see the papers in advance of the loan closing. Legitimate lenders are glad to co-operate.

Chances are that the lender may "give" some on the terms. Keep in mind also that, while you're mulling over the terms, you may want to get the advice of your associates and outside advisers. In short, try to get terms which you know your company can live with. Remember, however, that once the terms have been agreed upon and the loan is made (or authorized as in the case of SBA), you are bound by them.

Now you have read about the various aspects of the lending process and are ready to apply for a loan. Banks and other private lending institutions, as well as the Small Business Administration, require a loan application on which you list certain information about your business.

For purposes of explaining a loan application, this *Aid* uses the Small Business Administration's application for a small loan (SBA Form 6B)—one for $25,000 or less. The SBA form is more detailed than most bank forms. The bank has the advantage of prior knowledge of the applicant and his activities. Since SBA does not have such knowledge, its form is more detailed. Moreover, the longer maturities of SBA loans ordinarily will necessitate more knowledge about the applicant.

Before you get to the point of filling out a loan application, you should have talked with an SBA representative, or perhaps your accountant or banker, to make sure that your business is eligible for an SBA loan. Because of public policy, SBA cannot make certain types of loans. Nor can it make loans under certain conditions. For example, if you can get a loan on reasonable terms from a bank, SBA cannot lend you money. The owner-manager is also not eligible for an SBA loan if he can get funds by selling assets that his company does not need in order to grow.

When the SBA representative gives you a loan application, you will notice that most of its sections ("Application for Loan" —SBA Form 6B) are self-explanatory. However, some applicants have trouble with certain sections because they do not know where to go to get the necessary information.

"Section 3—Collateral Offered" is an example. A company's books should show the net value of assets such as business real estate and business machinery and equipment. *Net* means what you paid for such assets less depreciation.

If an owner-manager's records do not contain detailed information on business collateral, such as real estate and machinery and equipment, he sometimes can get it from his federal income tax returns. Reviewing the depreciation that he has taken for tax purposes on such collateral can be helpful in arriving at the value of these assets.

If you are a good manager, you should have your books balanced monthly. However, some businesses prepare balance sheets less regularly. In filling out "Section 7—Balance Sheet as of_____, 19___, Fiscal Year Ends_____" of the SBA loan application, remember that you must show the condition of your business within sixty days of the date on your loan application. It is best to get expert advice when working up such vital information. Your accountant or banker will be able to help you.

Again, if your records do not show the details necessary for working up profit-and-loss statements, your federal income tax returns (Schedule C of Form 1040, if your business is a sole proprietorship or a partnership) may be useful in getting together facts for Section 8 of the SBA loan application. This section asks for "Condensed Comparative Statements of Sales, Profits or Loss, etc." You fill in the blocks appropriate to your form of business organization—corporation, partnership, or proprietorship—and attach detailed profit-and-loss statements.

Insurance

SBA also needs information about the kinds of insurance a company carries. The owner-manager gives these facts by listing various insurance policies. If you place all your insurance with one agent or broker, you can get this information from him.

Personal Finances

SBA also must know something about the personal financial condition of the applicant. Among the types of information are: personal cash position; source of income including salary and personal investments; stocks, bonds, real estate, and other property owned in the applicant's own name; personal debts including installment credit payments, life insurance premiums, and so forth.

Once you have supplied the necessary information, the next step in the borrowing process is the evaluation of your application. Whether the processing officer is in a bank or in SBA, he considers the same kinds of things when determining whether to grant or refuse the loan. The SBA loan processor looks for:

(1) The borrower's debt-paying record to suppliers, banks, home mortgage holders, and other creditors.
(2) The ratio of the borrower's debt to his net worth.
(3) The past earnings of the company.
(4) The value and condition of the collateral that the borrower offers for security.

The SBA loan processor also looks for: (1) the borrower's management ability, (2) the borrower's character, and (3) the future prospects of the borrower's business.

How Much Interest?

What the preceding advisory didn't discuss—and couldn't —was the matter of how much interest you will have to pay. Rates vary so greatly that the fact of their variability is about all that can be stated for certain. *Prime interest* is the rate charged borrowers who have shown impeccable repayment habits, have vast holdings to secure the loan, and direct all kinds of other valuable business toward a bank. General Motors and American Tel and Tel are examples of prime borrowers. You are not likely to qualify for prime, although with the requirements above in mind, and on certain types of loans, you might qualify to borrow at .5 percent above prime.

Prime is generally set by big New York and Eastern banks and followed closely by banks in other sections of the country.

The point of mentioning prime is that, despite its applicability to only top-notch borrowers, *prime interest rates have varied by as much as 100 percent during as little time as five years!*

Other rates have varied still more. When banks have plenty of lendable money and relatively few borrowers, they extend near-prime rates to more people and companies, then jerk that favored rug away when their supplies of dollars are tight, so that a firm that might be borrowing near prime one year might be paying 2 or 3 percent over prime a year and a half later. This has happened. It is why non-prime rates varied by 200 percent over the same half-decade that saw prime jump and jiggle around by 100 percent.

I cannot tell you what interest rate you should pay—other than to become knowledgeable about prime (the *Wall Street Journal* and other business publications report prime rate changes regularly) and borrow as close to this magic, favored figure as you can. Remember the pointers discussed by the Small Business Administration experts quoted earlier.

However friendly your bank relations are, you should beware two words when you negotiate a loan. If your banker offers you money close to prime, that is good. If afterward, he murmurs, "compensating balance, of course," that is not good. Compensating balance means that you cannot use all of the funds you borrow but must pay interest on the whole amount.

Example: A firm borrowed $100,000 but agreed to maintain 20 percent compensating balance. That would mean $20,000 would be unusable. At prime rate of 8.5 percent charged on the full $100,000, the borrower would pay $8,500 but be able to use only $80,000. His effective rate would be 11.6 percent.

Beware another word—*discount.* It can make the true interest you pay higher than you would pay at simple interest. Look at the same $100,000 loan. Assume a two-year payout on a regular schedule of $12,500 per quarter. Interest would be payable quarterly. Average amount owed during the period would be approximately $50,000. Simple interest charged on this would mean high interest payments at first, with interest declining as the balance declined. It would run approximately $8,500 for the two-year period, or $4,250 yearly on the average.

If the banker were to make this a discount loan, however, he would compute interest for two years at the full amount, and deduct this off the top. He would then take $17,000 interest instead of $8,500. Moreover, since interest came off the top, the firm would only receive $83,000 instead of $100,000. Payments would be made quarterly, and the average balance payable during the period would be about $41,500. A quick computation of $17,000 interest over two years—$8,500 per year—on an average $41,500 balance yields an interest figure of 20.4 percent.

You have an absolute right to be told the facts about a loan before you sign any papers. This is guaranteed by federal law. The law is called "Truth in Lending." The Board of Governors of the Federal Reserve System, which oversees banking and financial matters everywhere in the United States, has an explanatory write-up called "What Truth in Lending Means to You." The Fed experts tell it this way:

> The law makes it easier for you to know two of the most important things about the cost of credit. One is the *finance charge*—the amount of money we pay to obtain credit. The other is the *annual percentage rate*, which provides a way of comparing credit costs regardless of the dollar amount of those costs or the length of time over which we make payments. Both the finance charge and the annual percentage rate must be displayed prominently on the forms and statements used by a creditor to make the required disclosures.
>
> Many of us know what interest is—6 percent per year for example. Let's suppose you borrow $100 for one year and pay 6 percent—or $6—for that money. If you have use of the entire amount for one year you are paying an *annual percentage*

rate of 6 percent. But if you repay the $106 in twelve equal monthly installments, you do not have use of the entire amount for the full year. In fact, over the entire year you have the use on the average of only about half the full $100. So the $6 charge for credit in this case becomes an *annual percentage rate* of 11 percent.

Some creditors levy a service charge or a carrying charge or some other charge instead of interest, or perhaps they may add these charges to the interest. Under the Truth in Lending Law they must now total all such charges, including the interest, and call the sum the *finance charge*. And then they must list the *annual percentage rate* of the total charge for credit.

The Truth in Lending Law does not fix interest rates or other credit charges. Your state may have a law setting a limit on interest rates, which would still apply.

One other important provision of the law is designed for your protection in case your home is used as collateral in a credit transaction. . . . When you enter into a credit transaction in which your home is used as collateral, the law gives you three business days to think about it and to cancel the transaction during that period if you wish. The creditor must give you *written notice of your right to cancel*, and if you decide to cancel the transaction, you have to *notify him in writing*.

Loans made during a period of very high interest rates, such as the nation went through in 1969 and 1970, can become costly and burdensome in later years when interest rates descend to lower levels. Periods of high interest rates are nearly always succeeded by low interest periods.

The point of mentioning this rather obvious fact is that it should be used as a guide in determining the length of a loan. Say you have to pay 11 percent because interest rates generally are high. It becomes to your advantage, then, to negotiate the loan for a short period. It is correspondingly to the banker's or other lender's advantage to stretch out the interest over as long a period as he can, since 11 percent loans are not a normal thing (although during recent spasms of tight money many raisers of small business capital had to pay this exorbitant rate—even higher on some occasions).

Better than a short-term loan would be one in which interest rates become negotiable every year or two. Either arrangement will prevent a costly drain on the business during future years. Such a drain is avoidable.

If you borrow during easy money times, it is advantageous, of course, to follow an opposite procedure, borrowing for as long a time as possible and avoiding any loan agreements that permit the lender to raise rates when it is to his interest to do so.

Something else to watch is the frequency of interest charges. One New York bank in 1972 began accumulating interest payments monthly on all of the loans where it was able to do so. Said a financial publication in commenting on this plan: "Adoption of such a system by other commercial banks across the country could have a broad impact on bank earnings and on corporate cash positions . . . [the decision] was based on a study which calculated that industry-wide adoption of monthly collections could mean additional $135 million of pretax earnings for the nation's more than 13,000 banks."

Guess out of whose pockets that $135 million will come. You won't need more than one try. Avoid this trap where you can, and be aware of its implications in all circumstances.

Be aware, too, of the trap inherent in another kind of bank loan. "Pays interest on checking accounts!" trumpets a typical ad. In the case of one Southern bank, it was set up this way:

If you kept $500 or more in the checking account—no charges, and payment of 5 percent interest.

If you wrote enough checks to drop the account down to $400 balance during the month—no interest paid, but 12 percent interest *charged* on the $100 "low" balance. You'd still have $400 on deposit with the bank, but you would pay out interest of $12 (annual rate) because your balance dropped below minimum. On *no loan*, interest is charged.

5: Uncle Sam Has Money for You

You have tried the borrowing sources mentioned earlier, and they have all told you: "You have a pretty good idea and we like it. But you haven't sufficient security. Sorry. No loan."

Banks are like that. They lend money, and when they do, they must be fairly certain, in fairness to the depositors whose money it is, that they can get it back. That's the first consideration—getting it back, as agreed, in full, and on promised time. A bank is not in the business of lending for ventures that, however worthy, do not have sufficient collateral to insure—or nearly insure—its prompt, timely, full repayment.

Happily, there is a lender that has been established by law to take chances a bank cannot take. It is called the US Small Business Administration. Congress established it to help people like you find the financing they need.

The preceding chapter took a brief look at SBA. Now we're going to examine this lender in greater detail. First, however,

62

let's take a look at the kind of business loans that the Small Business Administration does *not* make:

   A. If the company can get money on reasonable terms:

     (1) From a financial institution.

     (2) By selling assets that it does not need in order to grow.

     (3) By the owner's using, without undue personal hardship, his personal credit or resources of his partners or principal stockholders.

     (4) By selling a portion of ownership in the company through a public offering or a private placing of its securities.

     (5) From other government agencies that provide credit specifically for the applicant's type of business or for the purpose of the required financing.

     (6) From other known sources of credit.

   B. If the direct or indirect purpose or result of granting a loan would be to:

     (1) Pay off a creditor or creditors of the applicant who are inadequately secured and in a position to sustain a loss.

     (2) Provide funds for distribution or payment to the owner, partners, or shareholders.

     (3) Replenish working capital funds previously used to pay the owner, partners, or shareholders.

   C. If the applicant's purpose in applying for a loan is to effect a change in ownership of the business; however, under certain circumstances, loans may be authorized for this purpose, if the result would be to aid in the sound development of a small business or to keep it in operation.

   D. If the loan would provide free funds for speculation in any kind of property, real or personal, tangible or intangible.

   E. If the applicant is a charitable organization, social agency, society, or other nonprofit enterprise; however, a loan may be considered for a co-operative if it carries on a business activity and the purpose of the activity is to obtain financial benefit for its members in the operation of their otherwise eligible small business concerns.

F. If the purpose of the loan is to finance the construction, acquisition, conversion, or operation of recreational or amusement facilities, unless the facilities contribute to the health or general well-being of the public.

G. If the applicant is a newspaper, magazine, radio broadcasting or television broadcasting company, or similar enterprise.

H. If any substantial portion (50 percent or more) of the net sales of the applicant is derived from the sale of alcoholic beverages.

I. If any of the gross income of the applicant (or of any of its principal owners) is derived from gambling activities.

J. If the loan is to provide funds to an enterprise primarily engaged in the business of lending or investments or to provide funds to any otherwise eligible enterprise for the purpose of financing investments not related or essential to the enterprise.

K. If the purpose of the loan is to finance the acquisition, construction, improvement, or operation of real property that is, or is to be, held primarily for sale or investment.

L. If the effect of granting of the financial assistance will be to encourage monopoly or will be inconsistent with the accepted standards of the American system of free enterprise.

M. If the loan would be used to relocate a business for other than sound business purposes.

Now let's examine what the Small Business Administration *does* do—and how it does its thing—in the words of an expert. He is Robert L. Kiley, former Industrial Co-ordinator, Development Commission, Hamden, Connecticut, and now Executive Director of Salisbury Wicomico (Missouri) Economic Development. Writing in *Area Development*, December 1968, Mr. Kiley pointed out:

The first area of qualification is company size, by employment. If you have employed less than 250 people, including employees of affiliates, salesmen, etc., you are considered a small business. However, if your average four past quarters of employment was between 250 and 1,000, you may be considered a small or large business. This would depend upon your dominance within your product field and the employment standard size which the SBA has developed for your particular type industry.

The company must be "independently owned," which allows for sole proprietorship, partnership, corporation, and even as a subsidiary or affiliate of another company or group of companies.

By law, the SBA makes loans to small business concerns only when financing is not available to them on reasonable terms and conditions from other approved sources. The ability to repay any loan, of course, is also a consideration, along with a look at management's ability, the product, past performance, and future business growth projections.

The paperwork is not much more complex than any financial institution would require, and it is often helpful in giving you a good look at your company and its future goals. This is sometimes overlooked as you become involved with the daily operation of a going business, except when forced to evaluate your outlook while preparing annual statements or reports.

A total of $350,000 is the maximum allowable loan by the SBA under this program to any single project. This is 80 percent of the total cost.

If SBA people are satisfied about the loan, they can arrange to get you about 80 percent. Part of this might be carried by the bank that turned you down in the first place but which, with Small Business Administration backing, is now willing to take the risk.

The Small Business Administration has special programs in special areas. One of them is lending to minorities; this will be examined in detail in the chapter that follows. These are generally more liberal than the already liberal SBA terms. One was described in a release relating to veterans of the Vietnam conflict:

> The new assistance, which will make it easier for veterans to start and maintain businesses, is in response to President Nixon's recent call for renewed commitment by all federal agencies toward men and women who will have served in the armed forces anywhere in the world during the Vietnam period, which began August 5, 1964. An estimated 5.8 million such veterans have returned to civilian life to date.
>
> These veterans will now be eligible for business loans, federal government contracts, and management assistance under SBA programs that previously were restricted to socially or economically disadvantaged persons. . . .
>
> Under the expanded programs, honorably discharged Vietnam-era veterans are now eligible for:
>
> 1. *Economic Opportunity Loans* (EOL) of up to $50,000 for fifteen years at a low interest rate (under title IV of the Economic Opportunity Act of 1964).
>
> Criteria for such loans are more liberal than in other SBA lending programs, although the veteran still will be required to satisfy certain credit and character requirements and to furnish reasonable assurance that the loan will be repaid. Such loans are available to veterans who wish to expand an existing business or to establish a new business.
>
> As with all SBA loans, the EOL program is predicated on the assumption that the veteran cannot obtain financial assistance through his bank or other normal lending channels at reasonable terms, or cannot obtain funds under SBA's regular business loan program.
>
> Such a loan also assumes that the veteran does not have sufficient personal financial resources, i.e., is in a low-income status.
>
> Applicants may be sole proprietorships, partnerships, or corporations. Where there are two or more principals, the veteran must own at least 50 percent of the business.
>
> Since the Agency considers that proper management is necessary to a successful business, a condition of such a loan

may require that the veteran undertake management training or counseling if it is necessary.

2. *Federal Government Contracts*, under the SBA program that obtains for small businesses a fair share of purchases made by the government for goods and services.

Again, under the same program that previously has applied only to minorities and other disadvantaged persons, veterans are now eligible for federal contracts (under section 8(a) of the Small Business Act), commonly called "8(a)" contracts.

In such contracts, the SBA obtains from other federal agencies prime contracts suitable for small businesses and subcontracts them to small firms.

Once a veteran's firm is approved by SBA as to its financial status and performance capability, the Agency then locates and awards contracts that fit the firm's capabilities.

3. *Management and Technical Assistance* from private management consulting companies contracted by SBA to provide such assistance (under provisions of section 406 of the Economic Opportunity Act of 1964). Such counseling was previously available only to socially or economically disadvantaged persons and those in high unemployment areas. The new assistance follows a previous agreement between SBA and VA last August to help veterans receive schooling and training necessary for eligibility for SBA loans.

The expanded programs are designed to provide special assistance to Vietnam-era veterans. Such veterans are also eligible to receive all standard SBA services for small business—equity financing, long-term loans, government contracts, management and technical training, surety bonds, certificates of competency, lines of credit, federal regulation compliance, and other assistance.

Until recently, SBA assistance was not available for businesses connected with agriculture. No longer is this true. Here's how the agency itself describes the new set-up as applied to what it terms agribusinesses:

Under the new policy, small businesses in certain agriculture-related industries are eligible to apply directly to SBA for financial assistance. Certain farming and agriculture-related businesses may now apply for SBA assistance if their loan applications have been turned down by the Farmers' Home Administration or agencies of the Farm Credit Administration.

Several agriculture-related enterprises that provide services to the agriculture community or buy and sell or process, but do not grow agriculture commodities themselves, are eligible to apply directly to SBA for financial assistance. These include small businesses engaged in the following activities:

1. Purchase and resale of agriculture commodities.
2. Packaging, freezing, or processing of meats, fish, fruits, and vegetables.
3. Slaughter of livestock and poultry.
4. Purchase and operation of harvesting combines or other machinery, warehouses, cold storage plants, feed mills, etc.
5. Advisory assistance, such as farm management or landscaping.
6. Operations of a commercial feed yard.
7. Operation of a hatchery for the production of baby chicks for sale to others, provided that the hatchery purchases more than 50 percent of its eggs from others.

Other activities directly eligible are the trapping of lobsters, crabs, wild animals, and other game and the production of nursery crops, flowers, bulbs, and allied crops.

An additional group of farming and agriculture-related businesses whose normal channels of federal financial assistance are the Farmers Home Administration and agencies of the Farm Credit Administration, may now apply to SBA if they have first been turned down by FHA or FCA. These include businesses who have annual receipts of not more than $250,000, are not eligible to receive U.S. Department of Agriculture support payments or production loans, and are engaged in the production of mushrooms, fruits, vegetables, edible nuts, castor beans, and field crops. Other businesses which will now be eligible and for which size standards are being developed include those engaged in the following activities:

1. Operation of a hydroponic farm.
2. Production of fur-bearing animals.
3. Operation of dry-lot dairies.

4. Participation in beef cattle or dairy cow pools.

5. Production of bees and honey.

6. Oyster planting.

7. Operation of a hatchery for the production of baby chicks for sale to others.

SBA can guarantee a loan advanced by the bank, but not in excess of $350,000 or 90 percent of the bank loan, whichever is less. SBA may also participate with a bank in a loan, each lender advancing an agreed percentage of the total loan.

The following agricultural and agriculture-related activities are *not* eligible for SBA financial assistance:

1. The production of one or more crops currently eligible for support payments or production loans from the U.S. Department of Agriculture.

2. The production of livestock or poultry.

3. The production of fish, unless the production process or type of fish is novel, innovative, or experimental in nature.

Veterans interested in taking advantage of any SBA programs may apply in person, or telephone or write to the nearest SBA office. There are eighty-five such offices located in the principal cities of all fifty states and Puerto Rico and Guam; these cities are listed in Appendix 1.

Money for Export

Since a prime purpose of our government is to increase export sales of American firms while slowing down the imports that in recent years have been greater in dollar volume than U.S. sales abroad, financing a new (or existing) business that has export sales opens the door to a special kind of money raising. Experts of the Federal Reserve Bank of Richmond explained the workings of a DISC—Domestic International Sales Corporation—in that bank's June 1972 *Monthly Review*:

> Paralleling the decline in the U.S. trade position, and perhaps contributing to some of it, has been a continued rise in U.S. overseas production. U.S. firms have increasingly supplied

foreign markets through foreign-based subsidiaries. Foreign sales of overseas manufacturing affiliates of U.S. companies in 1970 were over twice the amount of direct exports of manufactured goods from the United States, and have grown about twice as fast as direct exports over the past decade.

U.S. exporters have operated under several handicaps in recent years. One of the most important has been domestic price and wage inflation, which, in addition to attracting increasing imports, has eroded the competitive position of some important U.S. exports in world markets. The U.S. trade surplus reached a peak of $6.8 billion in 1964 and then began to decline as inflationary pressures intensified. While demand inflation was brought under control in mid-1969, cost-push pressures continued to undermine the competitive position of U.S. exporters and domestic producers confronted with a challenge from imports. Reinforcing these pressures were the problems caused by having the cyclical positions of the United States and foreign countries out of phase. Of course, the realignment of exchange rates in 1971 was intended to compensate partially for this.

United States exporters have traditionally been able to compete effectively in world markets, despite relatively high U.S. wage levels, largely because productivity gains held down unit labor costs. In the early 1960s, labor costs per unit of output actually declined in the United States, while rising substantially in other major trading nations. From 1965 through 1970, however, unit labor costs in the United States rose more than 20 percent, which was above the average for this country's trading partners. This rise meant that higher wages were translated into higher, and often noncompetitive, export prices. The relative U.S. cost position improved in 1971, however, as inflation in Western Europe and Japan surged ahead of that in the United States, although there has not been sufficient time for this improvement to show up in the trade figures. The devaluation of the dollar should prove to be a more important immediate factor improving the relative U.S. cost position. . . .

Even though its efforts have lagged far behind foreign practices, the United States has taken some steps to encourage exports. The Department of Agriculture promotes U.S.

agricultural exports in various ways. The Department of Commerce and, to a more limited extent, other government agencies have various programs to encourage exports of manufactured goods. Its promotion efforts include numerous overseas commercial exhibits and trade missions abroad and marketing assistance and information to U.S. exporters and potential exporters.

The United States has also attempted to provide export financing on terms comparable to the favorable terms available to foreign exporters. The primary purpose of the Export-Import Bank is to encourage U.S. exports through its export financing programs. Its programs are intended to supplement and encourage private export financing rather than to compete with private sources. The Exim Bank guarantees and insures export credits extended by banks and other financial institutions, discounts their export paper, joins in cooperative financial arrangements, and extends direct credits out of its own resources. Under the auspices of the Export-Import Bank, the Foreign Credit Insurance Association—an association of private insurance companies—also insures export credits against commercial credit risks. The Department of Defense guarantees loans to foreign buyers of certain U.S. military goods. The Commodity Credit Corporation, an agency of the Department of Agriculture, conducts several export financing programs as a by-product of its function of supporting U.S. farm prices and disposing of U.S. agricultural surpluses abroad.

In an effort to facilitate export financing further, Congress, in the Export-Expansion Finance Act of 1971, removed Export-Import Bank disbursements from federal budget expenditures and expanded its lending capacity by about one-half. Increased borrowing and lending authority permitted expansion of the Export-Import Bank's discount program into short-term as well as medium-term export paper. Congress also removed export credits from the foreign lending ceilings applicable to banks and other financial institutions under the Voluntary Foreign Credit Restraint Program. Export credits guaranteed or participated in by the Export-Import Bank, insured by the Foreign Credit Insurance Association, or guaranteed by the Department of Defense were already exempt under the Voluntary Foreign Credit Restraint Program.

While the United States has provided favorable export financing, its export promotion efforts have fallen short of those of its main competitors. The United States' major trading partners spend roughly twice as much on export promotion in proportion to their exports as does the United States. Moreover, many countries' promotional efforts have been only one part of an integrated program of export expansion. The United States has relied more on its technological superiority to remain competitive in world markets. While this has sufficed in the past, recent experience suggests that it may not be sufficient in the future. In today's highly integrated world of multinational corporations, computerization, and rapid communication and transportation, technological advantages are short-lived. New realities have forced a reassessment of the U.S. competitive position and its approach to world competition in the future. With such considerations in mind, Congress included in the Revenue Act of 1971 an important program for export expansion. It provided for the establishment of Domestic International Sales Corporations, or DISCs. . . .

A DISC's operations are limited to export-related activities. Such a corporation may purchase export goods from its shareholders (parent firm) or other U.S. manufacturers and resell them abroad. Or a DISC may export for its suppliers as an agent on a commission basis. It may also lease or sublease U.S. property to foreigners. Although a DISC may not manufacture its own products for export, it may perform limited processing, packaging, or assembly operations on the products it sells. It may also render services in connection with its export transactions and perform a limited number of other services for foreign concerns.

A DISC itself is not subject to federal income tax on any of its profits. The tax is imposed on the shareholders, or parent firms, when the profits are distributed to them. The DISC shareholders are treated as having received half of the DISC's earnings currently, whether they are actually distributed or not. This half of the profit is deemed to be attributable to the manufacture of the product rather than its export. The remaining half, considered the export profits, may be retained by the DISC with no shareholder tax liability as long as those earnings are reinvested in its export business, invested in certain Export-Import Bank obligations, or loaned to U.S. producers to finance export-related assets. It is important to note that through these "producer's loans" the earnings of the DISC may be made available to its parent company or other export producers without sacrificing their tax-deferred status. If a foreign subsidiary made such a loan to its U.S. parent company, the loan would be taxed as a dividend. The shareholders of the DISC are taxed on the formerly deferred earnings when these earnings are distributed as dividends or when the corporation loses its status as a DISC. . . .

In order to qualify as a DISC, a corporation must derive at least 95 percent of its revenues from export sales and export-related investments, and 95 percent of its assets must be "export related." If a firm fails to meet these two crucial tests it can retain its status as a DISC by distributing its unqualified earnings or assets to its shareholders as a taxable dividend. Otherwise, it loses its status as a DISC. If a corporation ceases to be a DISC for any reason, its retained earnings become taxable to its shareholders over the same number of years as the DISC has been in existence, or a maximum of ten years.

As indicated above, a corporation must derive at least 95 percent of its gross receipts from exports or export-related activities to qualify as a DISC. Qualified receipts include receipts from the sale or leasing of export goods and the performance of related services, dividends from investments in qualified foreign sales subsidiaries, and interest income on any qualified export asset, such as accounts receivable from export sales, producer's loans, and Export-Import Bank obligations. Qualified receipts also include receipts from performing architectural and engineering services on foreign construction projects and from export management services provided for unrelated DISCs.

The DISC program is a tax shelter rather than direct financing. It is important to know about it nevertheless because, combined with sources of export financing mentioned in the Federal Reserve study, it can make such a program more profitable—therefore, more desirable as a risk to a lender or potential equity owner of the business you want to finance.

6: If You're a Member of a Minority

I_T is difficult in many ways in late twentieth-century America to be a minority member. But not when it comes to raising funds to start a new business or expand an existing one.

MESBIC to the Rescue

MESBIC is the largest and most active of the agencies devoted to helping minority members find the funds to build viable businesses. This is an arm of the Small Business Administration, at which we looked earlier. The initials stand for Minority Enterprise Small Business Investment Company. These SBICs will be examined in more detail—as they apply to *all* enterprises—in a coming chapter. MESBICs are a kind of Small Business Investment Company with a special slant toward members of ethnic minorities and other disadvantaged groups.

A series of questions and answers about MESBIC was posed by the Investment Division of the Small Business

Administration. Here's how the experts fielded the questions:

Small business investment companies—called SBICs—were created under the Small Business Investment Act of 1958 as a vehicle for providing equity capital and long-term loan funds for small businesses. The privately owned SBIC is licensed, regulated, and, in part, financed by the Small Business Administration. It makes equity investments in and long-term loans to small firms for the sound financing of their operations and for their expansion and modernization. The SBIC also provides management counseling and advice.

A MESBIC is a regular SBIC which has a strong parent support and a specialized investment policy of assistance to the disadvantaged.

MESBICs are, in effect, SBICs which specialize in providing equity funds, long-term loans, and management assistance to small business concerns owned by socially and economically disadvantaged persons. MESBICs are an integral part of the SBIC program and are governed by the same rules and regulations.

The MESBIC program is a private sector-government operation that has proven itself. Disadvantaged small businesses are being assisted. This flexible source of financing is proving its value to the nation's small businesses.

The MESBIC program is not a program of charity, grants, or giveaways, but a solid, businesslike solution to a great national economic and social problem.

The following series of questions and answers will help you better understand the MESBIC program.

What is an SBIC?

An SBIC is a privately owned and privately operated small business investment company. These companies were created under the Small Business Investment Act of 1958. They are licensed, regulated, and, in part, financed by SBA. They are a vehicle to provide equity capital and long-term loan funds for the nation's small businesses.

What is a MESBIC?

A MESBIC is a privately owned and privately operated SBIC dedicated to providing long-term funding and management assistance to disadvantaged small businessmen.

What is the difference between an SBIC and a MESBIC?

The investment policy plus the support of a strong parent.

What is a MESBIC investment policy?

The MESBIC agrees to provide financing to small business concerns that will contribute to a well-balanced national economy by facilitating ownership by persons whose participation in the free enterprise system is hampered because of social and economic disadvantages.

What is a strong parent?

A business, corporation, group, or organization that can provide the necessary financial backing and management assistance to the MESBIC and its portfolio companies.

What is a disadvantaged small business?

Generally, a small business concern that is at least 50 percent owned and managed by individuals from minorities that are underrepresented in the free enterprise system. The major eligible minority groups are American Negroes, Indians, Eskimos, and Aleuts, and Americans of Mexican, Puerto Rican, Cuban, Filipino, or Oriental extraction.

What is a small business?

In general, SBA considers a firm to be "small" if its assets do not exceed $5 million, if its net worth is not more than $2.5 million, and if its average net income after taxes for the preceding two years was not more than $250,000.

What are the capital requirements for forming a MESBIC?

The minimum private investment is $150,000. Where a minimum-size ($150,000) MESBIC is proposed, provisions should be made to cover the MESBIC's operating expenses without depleting its capital.

Can government funds or grants be used to capitalize a MESBIC?

No. Legislative history provides for maximum use of private funds and prohibits using an SBIC (MESBIC) as a mere conduit of government funds.

May government funds or grants be used to cover a MESBIC's operating expenses?

Yes, if not specifically prohibited by the terms of the grant.

What are the steps in setting up a MESBIC?

First, commit the necessary capital. Second, incorporate as an

investment company. Third, file the license application with
SBA.

What does a MESBIC application cover?

The application covers the basic corporate organization,
capitalization, operating and investment plans, and management. It also details the personal history of the officers, directors, and ten-percent owners of the MESBIC.

May a MESBIC specialize in a particular industry?

Generally, a MESBIC operates under a diversified investment policy with not more than one-third of its portfolio
comprised of investments in any one major industry group. A
MESBIC may specialize, however, provided a responsible
official of the MESBIC can demonstrate experience in the
field in which the MESBIC proposes to specialize.

May a MESBIC be used for real estate financing?

A new company will not be licensed if it proposes to put
more than one-third of its assets into real estate investments.
However, loans secured by real estate mortgages are not
counted as real estate investments if the proceeds of the loans
are to be used for purposes other than real estate investment.

*May a MESBIC provide financing to a small business concern
which is one of the principal suppliers of the parent of the MESBIC?*

Yes, with SBA approval.

*What are the basic regulatory features under which a MESBIC
must operate?*

MESBIC investments must be in small business.

MESBICs cannot invest more than 20 percent of paid-in
capital in any single small business concern.

MESBICs may not self-deal.

MESBICs may not take control.

MESBICs must operate according to their investment
policies.

What are the basic regulatory procedures?

In addition to an annual examination by SBA, each MESBIC
will file a semiannual unaudited financial report, an annual
audited financial report, and an annual portfolio company
information form.

What guides are available on regulatory aspects?

Every holder of a license to operate a MESBIC is furnished a guide to Small Business Administration regulations and automatically receives all amendments to the regulations, as well as policy and procedural releases which provide additional information.

Must a MESBIC be small and be owned by minority persons?

No. The larger the better, and it may be owned by corporations, community organizations, or otherwise.

Must paid-in private capital of a MESBIC be in cash, or may it be in mortgages or securities?

Cash or eligible government securities only.

Is there any restriction on a prospective stockholder of a proposed MESBIC borrowing funds for his investment in the MESBIC?

He may borrow funds for investment in the MESBIC if he can demonstrate a net worth equal to at least twice the amount borrowed.

May a MESBIC be publicly held?

Yes.

Will the operations of a MESBIC be exempt from Securities and Exchange Commission regulations?

Certain exemptions are available.

May a franchisor own and operate a MESBIC?

Yes, under certain conditions.

May a bank own a MESBIC?

A bank may own as much as 49.9 percent of any class of voting securities. Also, a bank may invest up to 5 percent of its paid-in capital and surplus in a MESBIC or MESBICs.

What office staff is required for a MESBIC?

At least one person comprising "qualified management," plus a secretary or assistant.

What leverage can SBA provide a MESBIC?

Generally, SBA can provide $2 of long-term subordinated government funds for every dollar of private capital, up to $7.5 million of government funds, and under certain conditions up to $10 million.

May a MESBIC borrow money for its operations from sources other than SBA?

Yes.

Can the small business concern that borrows from a MESBIC obtain other government financing?

Yes. A MESBIC financing does not preclude use of other available government funding by the disadvantaged small business concern.

Can the small business concern that borrows from a MESBIC obtain additional financing from private sources?

Yes. In fact, a MESBIC may take a subordinated position in its initial financing, thereby improving the credit position of the small concern for this very purpose.

Will SBA provide incentives to make additional private financings available?

Yes. SBA may guarantee up to 90 percent of a loan made by an institutional investor to a MESBIC portfolio concern.

What are the major tax advantages to a MESBIC?

MESBIC shareholder may treat gains on a sale of his stock as long-term capital gains.

MESBIC shareholder may take unlimited ordinary-loss deduction on losses relating to sale or exchange of his SBIC stock.

MESBIC may deduct 100 percent of dividends received from portfolio concerns.

MESBIC may be allowed unlimited ordinary-loss deduction rather than capital loss deduction on its investments.

Publicly held MESBICs and any other MESBICs registered with the Securities and Exchange Commission may "pass through" their income to shareholders in lieu of payment of corporate tax.

May a MESBIC extend financing to a small concern the controlling stockholders of which are also stockholders in the MESBIC?

Unless an exemption is granted by SBA, a MESBIC may not extend financing to a small concern with which an officer, director, or owner of 10 percent or more of the stock of the MESBIC is affiliated. The officer, director, or owner of 10 percent or more of the MESBIC would be considered affiliated with the small concern if he were an officer, director, or owner of 10 percent or more of the stock of such concern, or were a partner.

What is the maximum rate of interest a MESBIC may charge?

Fifteen (15) percent or rate permitted by state law,whichever is lower. In the calculation of the actual rate charged the borrower, SBA takes into account all charges, discounts, etc., and computes the rate on the basis of the outstanding balance.

Do SBA regulations cover the negotiations between the MESBIC and the borrower concerning types of loans, interest rates, discounts, and conversion features?

No. The relationship between the MESBIC and the client is entirely a private one, assuming, of course, that the transaction is in accordance with SBA's overall regulations and the intent of the program.

Is a MESBIC subject to any investment loan limitation?

Yes. Total funds guaranteed by, loaned to, or invested in equity securities may not exceed 20 percent of the paid-in capital and surplus of the MESBIC. Two or more MESBICs or SBICs may participate in a single investment, thereby providing a larger dollar total of financing in a single firm.

May the license of a MESBIC be transferred?

Yes, with prior SBA approval.

Is the stock of a MESBIC freely transferable?

Yes, but transfers of 10 percent or more must be approved by SBA.

Is there any restriction or limitation on the payment of dividends by a MESBIC while it remains indebted to SBA?

Yes. Where a MESBIC is indebted to SBA, dividends may be paid only out of retained earnings.

May a group of residents in one state incorporate the MESBIC under the laws of a neighboring state, and conduct the MESBIC's investment business in both states?

It depends upon the laws of the particular state.

May a MESBIC establish branch offices?

Yes.

May a MESBIC be converted to a regular SBIC?

Yes, with SBA approval.

What restrictions are there concerning the types of businesses to which loans may be made by a MESBIC?

A MESBIC may not provide funds to a small business

concern for relending, for purposes not contemplated by the Small Business Investment Act, or for purposes contrary to the public interest, such as gambling activities or fostering a monopoly. It may not provide funds for foreign investment, for agricultural enterprises, or for any business not conducted as a regular and continuous activity. Funds invested in real estate enterprises must not exceed one-third of a MESBIC's portfolio.

In addition to the rules and regulations of the SBA, are there any important rules or limitations concerning the number and the affiliations of the incorporators of a MESBIC?

The incorporators must conform to the laws of the state in which they propose to incorporate.

What do MESBIC administrators look for in making a loan? Study of some case histories can be helpful. Here are observations on some typical firms financed with MESBIC money:

1. *One-Day Delivery Service in the Bay Area*—This business presently has seven vehicles. The owner has hired an office manager and is now spending most of his time on sales. Hewlett-Packard has offered him some sales and management assistance and partial financing in conjunction with our financing. It will be two or three months before we know if the company is able to make a reasonable profit. Right now, the company employs nine men, five or six of whom were not previously employed in substantial steady work. The owner has demanded the best from them and has developed an exceptional record of reliability and good service.

2. *Bus Service*—The first several months of this operation were mainly training months for the owner. He has gained a relatively inexpensive education in the necessities of running a bus service and is now in the process of expanding his line by adding some diesel buses that will be less costly to operate. He is a competent manager and has an excellent chance to develop a reasonably good-sized charter service in the next three or four years.

3. *Furniture Restoration*—The furniture store has hired an

apprentice Mexican-American craftsman to learn the high-quality furniture business from the owner. In the next few months, he will also hire another skilled craftsman possibly from Southern California or Mexico. This businessman is thoroughly versed in his work. He has been most receptive to marketing and accounting aid and has been taking a business education night course offered by the Stanford Business School professors for minority businessmen.

4. *Beauty Shop*—The young owner of the beauty shop was careful and took his time to hire the best operators he could find. During the first three or four months he covered some of the overhead himself. Now the shop is operating quite profitably.

5. *Cleaners*—The young men who were originally financed in this business have sold it to an older couple. The husband works for the Post Office and the wife has been working in various cleaning establishments. The former owners made a small profit. It was best to have them sell out since the cleaning business was not exciting enough to suit their tastes. The new owners seem very enthusiastic with the business and have made excellent progress in just two or three weeks.

6. *Food Store*—Our only actual loss for the first year of operation was on this grocery store, one of the first businesses we financed. Unfortunately, our analysis was weak on two counts. First, we've come to realize that the attraction to the large supermarket chain is greater than we thought, and that even though the smaller market has convenience and sometimes equal or better service and prices, the customers are reluctant to leave the chain stores across the freeway. The second mistake was that the owner was not capable of developing an on-going relationship with customers and employees. Although he did a good job putting the store together, his immaturity showed up in the management of the business and eventually caused the failure. The business has been sold with a loss to a new, competent owner, who is now waiting for final legal arrangements to be closed so that he can develop his own style with the business. We will have to wait and see whether or not the business can succeed.

7. *Soul Food Take-Out*—The owner, a very good business-woman, and her husband, an experienced carpenter, have developed from almost nothing a very pleasant and sizable take-out restaurant. Their line has expanded to serve most typical soul food items as well as ice cream, soft drinks, hamburgers, and milk shakes. The business has been exceptionally profitable and continues to grow.

8. *Janitorial Service*—The growth of the first building maintenance company that we financed has been less promising than we had hoped. The owner has continued to keep his other job and has not put in the time necessary to make the business really go. On the other hand, he has developed, on a small basis, a good reputation and has a good base for growth that will be helpful when he decides that he wants to devote full time to the business. His main interest seems to be starting a maintenance supply store.

9. *Printing Company*—The printing company has been one of the most successful ventures to date, although it is not quite at the breakeven point. In the first six months of operation, we thrashed through considerable disorganization and lack of productivity, the results of the business being set up too fast and too large. The printing company has now begun to close the gap between sales and cost at an extremely rapid pace. The fifteen-man force is capable and well organized, and the company continues to increase its sales through the efforts of two newly trained salesmen. The president of the company is an exceptional manager and has been able to develop a high level of morale while at the same time being a tough manager, replacing those people who are not able to deliver. This business, one of our biggest to date, was a good lesson in the necessity of starting any business in a fairly typical or natural growth pattern. Forty- or fifty-employee businesses do not generally start at that size; they must grow from a smaller shop.

10. *Restaurant in Mall Complex*—The restaurant is not yet open. Delays have been caused by poor planning on the construction phases of the business and the typical delays of starting any new business. We will not know for several months whether the business will be successful, but we have become increasingly convinced that there is excellent potential for this

restaurant. It is being put together in a very professional manner.

To many people, "minority" means "black." This is not true of SBIC and MESBIC lending practices. As Thomas S. Kleppe of the U.S. Small Business Administration explained in a 1972 advisory:

> Small business investment companies (SBICs) and minority enterprise small business investment companies (MESBICs) may now make venture capital investments in new finance and insurance small business concerns owned by *socially or economically disadvantaged persons.*
>
> The expansion of investment opportunities is possible under a new SBA rule amending SBIC regulations.
>
> Security brokers and dealers, insurance companies, federally insured savings and loan associations, mortgage bankers, credit companies, and other lenders, with the exception of commercial banks, savings banks, and agricultural credit companies, will be eligible for the new venture capital financings to the extent of the SBICs' and MESBICs' private paid-in capital and paid-in surplus.
>
> It is expected that this liberalization will fill a specific gap in the minority community by assisting disadvantaged persons in starting and maintaining financially oriented small business concerns and provide a funnel through which funds can flow and generate increased economic activity.

A list of local Minority Enterprise Small Business Investment Companies can be had by contacting local offices of the U.S. Small Business Administration, the locations of which are given in Appendix 1. Addresses of MESBICs are given in Appendix 2.

Non-governmental Monetary Aid for Minorities

Once fearful of non-majority enterprises and scornful of minority abilities to pull off a projected deal, Establishment businessmen are now becoming aware of this area of responsibility and—more important in a capitalistic society—of opportunity.

Edwin C. Gooding, economist at the Federal Reserve Bank of Boston, explained it in an article in the Bank's *New England Review*:

> Hopefully, all of us feel some personal motivation and desire to eliminate racial inequality and injustice that no truly civilized society can tolerate. But even if personally motivated, the chief executive of a large, profit-seeking firm may be hard pressed to justify expending any significant amount of his corporation's resources toward a social goal such as racial equality. He may ask, "Isn't that the government's responsibility?" The achievement of all forms of racial equality must be everyone's responsibility—a governmental effort will not be enough.
>
> The president of each large firm represents a critical power point in our society. Unless many of these points are activated to do something positive in the area of black-white relations, our society will continue to be disrupted by sporadic and costly violence stemming from past and present racial injustice. Thus sharply increased expenditures by business in the area of black-white relations ought to be viewed as a real effort to insure a social climate where it is possible to do business as usual.
>
> Once you, as a corporate leader, become concerned, you then may be dismayed to find that there are many challenges: employment, training, education, black capitalism, and police-community relations are but a few areas involving black-white relations. How many of these challenges you can accept will vary with the skills and resources of your company. . . .
>
> Black capitalism is a tangible form of self-help and is not identical with black separatism. If a black can keep part of his income "circulating within the community" by "buying black," this will, indeed, help raise income levels somewhat. On the other hand, most black businessmen realize that limiting their customers to blacks is unprofitable, if not suicidal.
>
> Let us recognize that in the battle for the minds of black youth, the image of a man who makes his living "in the street"

can compete quite effectively with that of the man who comes home with a lunch box from a job as a janitor. Our society must demonstrate that ownership of business is not a privilege limited to whites. Successful black businessmen can be examples of men who can "make it big" legitimately within the confines of the ghetto. . . .

Let us assume that you decide to assist the black capitalism movement in some way. There are some operating rules that I have found useful and which may improve the effectiveness of your efforts.

To be successful you must be willing to go more than half-way in any black-white relationship. In our society, any black-white relationship cannot be truly color-blind. The past three hundred years have left subtle marks upon us all. A successful interracial relationship calls at first for more sensitivity to the race issue, not less. The executive must be aware that others on his staff may be less than eager to implement his recommendations. We must make a massive effort if we are going to enable blacks to rapidly overcome the impact of over three hundred years of subjugation and second-class citizenship. However, as you bend over backwards, you must do it in such a sophisticated manner that only the most observant will notice, an admittedly difficult task.

Another useful operating principle is that, even though you do bend over backwards, you should not believe the rhetoric that tells you that the laws of economics do not apply in the ghetto. Do not accept economic or business nonsense just because the spokesman happens to be black. Businesses must still meet a payroll in the ghetto. Most of the problems of black capitalism are the same problems confronted by any small business: under-capitalization, insufficient management know-how, inadequate marketing strategies, and so forth. Added to these problems are those associated with low income areas, such as the generally more limited income of customers and a higher incidence of crime. . . .

Many individuals outside the banking community have said, in effect, "It does not take much commitment for banks to make a black business loan when it has a 90 percent or 100 percent guarantee against default." Such a statement could not be further from the truth. Most loans to black businesses would not be made if the loan officer approached the loan on a strictly color-blind basis. An effective commercial bank minority loan program requires a great deal more staff time than is required to make a similar volume of conventional loans. Consequently, the level of commitment of a commercial bank to the black capitalism movement is best measured by the amount of staff time freed to make—and service—minority loans, rather than by the volume of uninsured minority loans it may have made. The designation of one or more loan officers as minority business loan specialists is one technique that may help to provide the bank with an efficient—and consistent—minority loan program.

We don't expect 100 percent success with "majority" business loans. Obviously, we should not expect such a record in minority loans. In fact, it is much more difficult for a business to survive in the ghetto than outside it. Vandalism, theft, and fire are more constant threats to all businessmen in the ghetto than to the businessmen operating in higher income areas. Although every business proposition funded should have a fighting chance for success, we should recognize that most large businesses today were built from a few firms that survived—and that many more firms tried and failed. In this respect, black capitalism should not be expected to evolve much differently from the way white capitalism did. . . .

A large corporation can aid the black capitalism movement by diverting some of its purchases from usual channels to products of black businesses. Buying or subcontracting from black businessmen is not easily done; nevertheless, it can be done with creative effort. One of the leaders in this type of purchasing is Western Electric, a company that according to a *Business Week* report has lined up over seventy minority suppliers. In order to do this, however, they have had to provide many potential suppliers with management and technical assistance—and, sometimes, even start-up capital.

Trade credit is one of the most difficult types of credit for a new black businessman to obtain, despite the fact that credit may be vital to his success. Perhaps your firm could follow the example of some members of the Menswear Retailers of

America, who have provided both regular and extended credit to black merchants throughout the country.

Corporations can also provide technical assistance to minority businessmen. Loans to aspiring black capitalists must be supported by management counseling if a significant number of these ventures are going to succeed. Many black businessmen who have come through our office have received technical assistance from us and from volunteers recruited from a pool of talented—and concerned—individuals. Some of these businesses are now well on their way to success—and it is likely that some of these same firms would have failed without outside technical help.

Not merely in New England, but all over the U.S. as well, large firms have responded to this appeal. General Foods Corporation, for example, in one reported case arranged a loan of nearly $30,000 to help out a black owner of a taxi fleet in trouble. Ford Foundation has appropriated money for the assistance of minority enterprises that without it could not get off the ground. A MESBIC sponsored by Arcata National Corporation, a California-based information firm, has been a sizable source of minority funds.

A key to all of this minority financing is in the phrase used by Edwin S. Gooding in his report: "Most loans to black businesses would not be made if the loan officer approached the loan on a strictly color blind basis."

Here is a report on what is being done in one large city, Philadelphia. It appeared in an article by Kathryn L. Kindl in the *Business Review* of the Federal Reserve Bank of that city:

> Which Philadelphians help?
>
> Government functions as a leader and catalytic agent. Through agencies such as the Small Business Administration and the Model Cities program, it provides financial resources and coordinating mechanisms. Financial institutions furnish risk capital, emphasizing the client's motivation and similar personal qualities. Other organizations—for example, Greater Philadelphia Enterprises Development Corporation (GPEDC) and Businessmen's Development Corporation (BDC)—offer

professional advice and consulting services. Franchisers take on black owner-operators, while other businesses tender special considerations in procurement. Many individual executives offer their expertise through volunteer counseling pools, such as the one maintained by GPEDC. The academic community provides educational resources through both student and faculty participation. Finally, community groups, including Mantua Community Planners, Inc., Young Great Society, and the Urban Coalition, work to open needed communication lines between the black and white communities and to muster local enthusiasm and support.

While capital for a new business is always hard to find, difficulties are compounded for minority businessmen. Traditional credit channels, which require a borrower to have some of his own financial resources, are closed to the black with no equity capital. In addition, inexperience or previous failures may handicap the Negro in need of financial backing.

Groups in Philadelphia are responding to these credit problems. First, some organizations provide pre-loan assistance and direct the potential businessman to a loan source. Second, many of these groups and others have established funds of capital for loan in high-risk situations.

The potential businessman may approach a lending agency, often after having been refused a loan via conventional channels, with the aid of a group such as Greater Philadelphia Enterprises Development Corporation or Businessmen's Development Corporation. These organizations examine the proposed project, developing, in the process, background information useful to the lender. They then refer the client to the most suitable loan source.

Initial screening by the organizations is designed to weed out unrealistic proposals. Applicants who survive this process benefit from comprehensive professional evaluation. The staffs of GPEDC and Job Loan and Urban Venture Corporation (JL&UVC), among others, thoroughly scrutinize each proposition for its technical feasibility. The location under consideration, proposed scale of business operations, and capital requirements are all examined with an expertise the inexperienced rarely possess. In the course of such an inquiry, suggestions may be made to improve the prospectus, and the entrepreneur often will be alerted to previously unforeseen difficulties.

Once the evaluation has been completed, the client will be referred to one of several loan sources—perhaps a commercial bank, Job Loan and Urban Venture Corporation, or the Small Business Administration. The organization responsible for initiating the borrower-lender relationship may help prepare the loan application and other necessary papers. A staff member of GPEDC or SBA often will accompany the applicant to the lending institution. Efforts are also made to have an accountant present in order to avoid later financial difficulties caused by misunderstanding.

In Philadelphia, commercial-bank money is available directly, with or without a government guarantee, and indirectly, through a special pool of bank funds—Job Loan and Urban Venture Corporation. Many clients go straight to the bank after screening and pre-loan assistance by organizations such as BDC and GPEDC. Other would-be businessmen, often designated as higher risk borrowers, are referred to JL&UVC. Through this nonprofit group, originally established in April 1968 as Job Loan Corporation, eight banks pool the higher-than-average risks associated with many loans to minority businessmen. Programs of the Small Business Administration (for example, Operation Business Mainstream, and its predecessor, Project OWN) also help break the ice at the commercial bank by offering the institution a federal guarantee of the loan. . . .

One additional source of capital is the black community itself. An example of the way in which minority businessmen may draw upon this economic base is the self-help experience of Zion Investment Associates. In 1962, the Reverend Leon Sullivan, pastor of the Zion Baptist Church, asked fifty members of his congregation to pool ten dollars a month for thirty-six months in an investment cooperative plan. For the first sixteen months this money was to be placed into a nonprofit charitable trust. The contributions of the final twenty months were put into an investment corporation for profit-making purposes. The Reverend Sullivan's pleas drew over two hundred responses, and Zion Investment Associates was on its way to launching the Progress Plaza shopping center, Progress Garment Manufacturing Company, and Progress Aerospace Enterprises, Inc. . . .

Although the sums of money lent minority businessmen vary within a wide range and are influenced by the character of the lending institution and the requirements of the entrepreneur, the average black business loan comes to about $15,000. For example, in its two and one-half year history, GPEDC has been instrumental in the approval of approximately fifty small business loans averaging between $15,000 and $20,000.

Black Banks

A final source of financing for blacks is the black community itself. There is a growing number of black-owned banks devoted to the opportunities found in financing minority businesses.

Reporting on these banks, Donald L. Kohn of the Federal Reserve Bank of Kansas City noted:

> The basic goals of a minority bank are no different from those of any other bank. Profits, which are necessary to attract capital so the firm can survive and expand in a market economy, are of primary importance. Clearly, profits will be enhanced by the efficient provision of banking services and the growth of deposits and assets in the bank. An important method of meeting the goal of growth is help to businesses in the bank's service area.
>
> For minority banks a legacy of discrimination and an environment of poverty compound the difficulty and importance of reaching these goals. Nationally, average black income is only 60 percent of average white income. Even more troublesome is that average black holding of liquid assets, such as savings and checking accounts, are only 19 percent of the average for whites. The region covered in this study is no exception to this pattern. In St. Louis, for example, the median income for nonwhite families was 58 percent of the median for all families in 1959. These factors handicap the deposit growth of minority

banks and contribute to high delinquency and loss ratios on their loans. Conditions are no better among the Spanish-American customers of Centinel Bank of Taos. Taos County, whose population is 70 percent Spanish surnamed, had a per capita income of $1,400 in 1967, which was only 44 percent of the average for the United States. Furthermore, incomes of the Spanish-Americans in the Taos area are probably lower than is indicated since this average is pulled up by relatively prosperous artists, white retirees, and owners of expanding tourist and ski industries.

Minority bankers attach extra significance to the attainment of their goals because of what it would demonstrate to other segments of society. A profitably run bank serving minorities might induce white bankers to make more credit available to minority communities. Several of the bankers interviewed stated that after their banks were opened marked changes were evident in the attitudes of white bankers toward minority employees and the desirability of minority banking business.

The bankers also felt that successfully operating within established social guidelines would have positive effects on their own people, especially the youth. They reasoned that a successfully run minority bank, financing successful minority owned businesses, would be a powerful force in overcoming the feelings of inferiority and futility they believe to be widespread among their people.

7: Love It and Lease It

IT is contrary to the traditional American notion of thrifty living to lease things in preference to owning them. The Horatio Algerites will tell you that it is better to save your money slowly, buy things a little at a time, pay for them in cash rather than debt, and finally end up with a list of possessions owned totally and in perpetuity.

Three cheers.

The cheers are for thrift, not for financing good sense. The fact is that leasing, in today's sophisticated world, is not a way of squandering but of borrowing money.

Leasing is a type of financing, an effective type able to advance not part, or most, but all of the funds needed for certain specific purposes. Leasing also confers certain tax advantages. It is a method of financing fully as important as borrowing from a bank, going public, seeking government funds, or any of the other ways available to raise money for starting a new business and expanding an existing one.

Leasing is a hot industry. You can lease a car, a building, a piece of equipment, all of your needs or some of them or

94

none of them. There are contracting firms that lease all they are able to, others that lease some things, still others that regard the whole question of leasing in somewhat the light that a pampered house cat would regard a large, growling neighborhood dog waiting outside.

The question is complicated. There is no standard way things are leased—not even the same things. You can rent any given piece of equipment with or without maintenance, or with partial maintenance. You can lease it by the month, year, two years. You can get a lease on land and put up your own building. You can obtain leases that have the option of becoming purchase contracts. These things vary with the lessee, the type of thing being leased, and most of all with the wishes and needs of the firm doing the leasing.

There is no right or wrong general answer to this question of leasing versus ownership. But for every particular fundraiser, there can be an answer that is advantageous in his particular circumstances. Looking over a list of pro and con points can help to clarify a decision.

Consider these points:

Pro: There is a big tax advantage. Often when you own something, you have to depreciate it for tax purposes on a lengthy table so that the cost is recovered only slowly. A lot of bookkeeping has to be done to obtain a tax saving, which is occasionally minuscule. If inflation proceeds at the same pace as in recent years (it is likely to get worse, not better), the tax saving becomes one of decreasingly valuable dollars as the depreciation table stretches into the future. Despite current efforts to contain the fires of inflation, there is no real reason to expect that these can be kept wholly under control over the longer term.

Leasing expenses do not have to be depreciated, stretched out, held to future years, or back-charged to years gone by. In general (there may be special cases on which your tax accountant can advise you), every cent put out for rent becomes a deduction in the year when it is expended.

Pro: Maintenance is decreased, sometimes eliminated. I discussed this question with an official of one leasing company. "We rent things either with or without maintenance contracts," he told me. "If you have a maintenance contract, we do everything. It is our piece of equipment, and we keep it in shape for you. No fuss, muss, wear, tear, or bother. No maintenance crew. In effect, the lessee rents our maintenance crews when he rents an item with maintenance contract."

It is well to understand that not all maintenance contracts are as thoroughgoing as the one this man described. Some contracts call for upkeep only on certain kinds of breakdowns, leaving other repairs to the lessee.

Pro: Fixed assets can become capital. Need money for expansion? For an acquisition? To take advantage of a special opportunity? Money that might be tied up in bricks, mortar, land, or equipment can be quickly freed by a contractor who chooses to go the leasing route.

Pro: Consolidation of accounts. With equipment you own, cost is amortized on the books under a depreciation account. Repairs or routine service to the equipment goes onto another account. When you pay taxes, a third entry is made. The salaries of men who keep equipment running go on a fourth account. One beauty of the leasing idea, according to many of its advocates, is that all these accounts and diverse entries are eliminated. Only rental must be entered.

"It's the lessor's equipment, not mine," shrugged one contractor. "In these days when it is so hard to get or to keep good clerical help, I am delighted to let him do all the paper work."

Pro: Early obsolescence isn't your worry. Some things are made quickly obsolescent by advancing technology. If a sizable write-off were to be made under those circumstances, profits might be penalized severely. "But when something gets out of date I call the leasing company, tell a man there, 'Hey, Joe—come get it and give us the later model,' and then the obsolescence problem is his," reported one businessman.

"Of course," he added, "not all leasing contracts contain provisions for this. If you want the obsolescence provision, as we do, you have to negotiate it into the contract and pay extra for it."

Pro: You are not tied down when a need ceases. Times change, people come and go. The need for a piece of equipment or a parcel of land, even for a building and certainly for the people who render contract services, can be altered totally. If you own things, or have a carefully trained staff of your own, then you are not in as good a position as the fellow who can shrug off the change, return equipment to a lessor, or wait out a lease expiration on real estate.

"Leasing," one of its strong advocates claims, "allows flexibility that would be impossible with ownership."

Pro: The payroll is usually smaller. This is obviously true in the case of contract services such as office help, for which you assume no Social Security or tax record problems, or the recruitment and payment of personnel. It is equally true in the case of a rented building or rented equipment where maintenance goes with the contract.

One smaller firm reported that saving in this direction was considerable. "I had to have certain specialized technicians on call and therefore on the payroll," the general manager said. "In consideration of our size, we did not need all of them all of the time. Now we rent. The lessor can spread his maintenance people over many contracts, and the same man who was sitting idle part of his time when on my payroll may now be servicing equipment at two or three scattered places. The contractor saves, and so do we."

Pro: Costs become fixed and predictable. Say you own certain machines. For many years they require only routine services. Then they have a spate of breakdowns. You don't know on January 1 whether the twelve months ahead are going to be a mechanically smooth period or whether the equipment is going to obey Murphy's Law (which states that if something can go wrong, it will). With equipment rented on service maintenance, your costs are fixed and known on January 1. It is the leasing contractor who has to worry whether Murphy's Law will be in effect in the year ahead.

The points above are impressive. But like most listings of advantages, they are not the whole story. Against those plus points of leasing, there are many points in favor of ownership and against the leasing concept. Specifically, you should bear in mind these drawbacks to the rental of buildings, equipment, and office or other specialized services:

Con: At the end of the lease period you have won nothing. Reduce the leasing question to the small matter of an automobile. On the day this was written, I investigated the cost of leasing versus buying a new model, four-door automobile in the middle price range.

With trade-in on an average three-year-old car it could have been purchased, loaded with air conditioning, power steering, power brakes, and radio, for about $4,400. Added to that over the cost of leasing would be the recurring charges for lube jobs, oil changes, tire and battery replacement, and the other things routinely needed with a car. On a full maintenance contract that furnished everything except gasoline, this same car could have been rented for about $160 monthly. On a two-year contract that came to $3,840, approximately the same amount as if the car had been purchased and maintenance costs assumed.

On a rental deal, the user of the car would possess nothing when his lease expired. On a purchase deal he would still be owner of a two-year-old automobile.

Change "automobile" to almost any item rentable and you have the idea.

Rentals are often designed to amortize buildings and equipment over the life of a lease.

Con: Suppose the asset has increased rather than depreciated in real value. This happens when prices of new equipment move up sharply or the equipment becomes hard to get. The older item may have a higher real present value than its cost. When items are rented, this occasional increase accrues to the lessor, not the lessee.

Con: You lose the bookkeeping item of depreciation. Depreciation in some instances can be as important as rental outgo in computing taxes. Your accountant or tax adviser should be consulted on this point before you assume that leasing always offers a savings. This is true particularly with real estate, where heavy early depreciation charges can turn ordinary income into eventual capital gains should a fully amortized building be sold when it no longer has depreciation usability.

"Unless there is a substantial tax saving to the lease idea—and there is not always one—then a lease becomes a financing gimmick," points out an accountant.

Con: A consolidated account sometimes costs more than many scattered small ones. This occurs when packaged charges for services exceed what a firm might expect to pay if it were able to bargain for service with separate outside people.

Con: You lose control over the speed and quality of maintenance services. "When something breaks down, I want it fixed—fast," says one small contractor. "Sometimes the lessor's maintenance services don't provide for speed. They almost never provide for bringing in men on overtime periods such as weekends or night hours when we might desperately need service."

Another complaint is that the lessor's services are not always of a quality comparable to that given by independent service people who must please their customers every time or see those customers switch to competitors.

So, is leasing intrinsically better than buying? There is one right answer for each firm, even though there is not a right or wrong way to do things applicable to all. Study of the pro and con factors may bring into focus that right decision for your company. Some have found that the lease agreement with option to purchase later offers the best of both approaches.

While all of those pros and cons are important, the overriding consideration for one in need of funds to start a new business or expand an existing one is, *leasing can raise money for your business.*

How this works in a typical case was explained to health professionals in the December 1971 issue of *Dental Economics* by Gerson E. Lewis, president of Medical Leasing Corporation of Skokie, Illinois. Mr. Lewis wrote for dentists. What he had to say is as applicable to contractors, shoe store owners, wholesalers, newsdealers, or any of the other myriad people who seek money for business (and professional) operation. Wrote Mr. Lewis:

> Railroads do it. Truckers do it. Hospitals do it. Ditto airlines. Why not the dentist?
>
> Lease equipment, that is.
>
> United Airlines recently leased six DC-8 jets, and it was a good deal for both the airline and the leasing company. The leasing company received cash flow by taking the depreciation credit, and the airlines took delivery of the jets without tying up a cent.
>
> TWA accepted $146 million worth of equipment in the same kind of a deal. United Tankcar has been leasing equipment to haul oil, chemicals, and cement for years.
>
> "Big corporations know when it is advantageous to lease," says Donald H. Metz, author of a manual entitled *Leasing Standards and Procedures. . . .*
>
> By 1970, the yearly leasing total hit approximately $6 billion; back in 1967, but three years before, only $1.3 billion worth of equipment was leased.
>
> And now I feel it's time . . . to give some serious thought to the advantages of leasing.
>
> A considerable amount of very expensive equipment is required in your . . . office. You may have to furnish multi-unit operatories, a laboratory, and a business office—and the financial requirements . . . can become quite extensive.
>
> Today you can acquire much needed equipment in three ways: You can pay cash. You can finance through bank loans. Or you can lease.

The first method of acquiring equipment—cash—is probably the best if you have surplus cash. However, it might be wiser to utilize the surplus cash for investment in a second asset that would be more productive than equipment. You might possibly consider an investment in a tax-shelter device to preserve the income that is earned from the equipment.

The second method of acquiring equipment—bank borrowing—is competitive in cost with leasing. However, there are some distinct disadvantages in borrowing from a bank. For example, these loans could tie up your credit line; if you needed additional funds to take advantage of a good real estate investment, you might find the bank reluctant to negotiate another loan. And your bank loan must be repaid with after-taxes "hard" dollars, with the interest being the only deduction during the term of the loan. The higher the tax bracket you are in, the more costly this type of borrowing becomes.

The third way to acquire equipment, via leasing, appears on the surface to be more expensive than bank borrowing. However, when you compare leasing to borrowing from a bank, you will find that leasing gives 100 percent financing where bank borrowing is controlled by the amount of equity required by the lender. The payments made during the term of the lease are completely tax deductible, which means you are paying with pre-tax "soft" dollars. Now, if your leasing company is knowledgeable and surrounds the leasing package with a form of all-risk insurance built into the rate, you will see that the insurance premium is deductible as well.

Lease terms of sixty to ninety-six months are usually recommended. This approaches the IRS guidelines for depreciation. There should never be a purchase option, either in a lease contract or in a side agreement. You may, however, purchase the equipment at fair market value after the termination of the lease.

Leasing gives . . . a way to obtain the newest equipment on the market. The lease contract should specify that the [lessee] may trade in or add to the contract at his desire. This means that as technological improvements occur, they are available . . . immediately, without consulting budget or cash resources. They can simply be added to the existing lease contract.

Another important advantage is the opportunity . . . to completely control budgetary and actual expenses for equipment.
This type of tight control is required . . . to operate . . .
efficiently. . . .

A possibility is a service covering the acquisition of any and
all types of new equipment. . . . [You] can procure all the
equipment necessary. . . . The benefits of the latest improvements are immediate. . . . [You] may select . . . from the
supplier of choice. When the equipment is satisfactorily installed and . . . approved, the leasing corporation "pays the
bills." Again, this leasing plan has rental payments which can
be customized to meet . . . needs.

A third option is a purchase and leaseback plan tailored to
the needs of the established practitioner (or firm). Participation
allows him to recover and better utilize capital presently
invested in equipment and furnishings. We all know this is a
more significant consideration than the tax benefits realized
from equipment depreciation. The purchase-leaseback plan
releases cash for investment while providing a tax benefit
inherent in equipment leasing. The leasing corporation will
purchase the existing equipment and lease it back to [you]. . . .
[You] remain in full use and control of equipment—without
a capital investment.

Each of these plans must be specifically tailored to the circumstances of the individual. In many cases the purchase-
leaseback plan must be tied in with a loan because there would
be ordinary income on the recapture of depreciation. For this
reason, a "lendlease" program is suggested as most beneficial.

The accompanying table shows the effects of a $20,000 sale-
and-leaseback plan and the net gains obtained through
leasing. . . .

The basic advantages of leasing are obvious—conservation of
capital and protection against inflation. Each year you pay with
cheaper dollars. You also have the opportunity to keep your
office equipment up to date, and you may possibly qualify for
reimbursement benefits when expenditures are accurately
controlled.

Leasing is not for everyone. But you should explore all the

possibilities to determine if this vehicle can be adapted to your advantage.

SALE AND LEASEBACK

Assumptions: $20,000 sale and leaseback, depreciated value on books is $10,000, purchased since 1962, 5-year lease, $10,000 gain in ordinary income (IRS section 1245)

Tax Bracket	40%	50%	60%	70%	80%
Sale of Equipment	20,000	20,000	20,000	20,000	20,000
Depreciated value	10,000	10,000	10,000	10,000	10,000
(Ordinary income)	10,000	10,000	10,000	10,000	10,000
Amount of tax	4,000	5,000	6,000	7,000	8,000
Net cash received	*16,000(A)*	*15,000(A)*	*14,000(A)*	*13,000(A)*	*12,000(A)*
Total rental payments	31,200[1]	31,200[1]	31,200[1]	31,200[1]	31,200[1]
Tax Deductions	12,480	15,600	18,720	21,840	24,960
Net cash cost over five years	*18,720*	*15,600*	*12,480*	*9,360*	*6,240*
Cost to obtain cash per year (B) minus (A)/5 yrs.	544	120	0	0	0
6% annual growth value on cash received	21,408	20,070	18,733	17,394	16,056
Cost (B)	*18,720*	*15,600*	*12,480*	*9,360*	*6,240*
Gain by sale and leaseback	2,688	4,470	6,253	8,034	9,816

[1] Includes life, accident and health, and all-risk insurance.

It is important to remember about leasing that it is *100 percent financing*. If you buy a typical lot of equipment you might put 25 percent down and be able to finance (borrow) the rest. If you lease it, you put nothing down.

One form of leasing gives you something back. If you already own land or buildings on which you plan to operate the projected business, you should be aware of sale-leaseback.

Sale-Leaseback

Put simply, sale-leaseback works this way: You sell your land or land plus buildings to a company, taking back an immediate long-term lease that guarantees that you can carry on right at the same old stand with the customers knowing nothing of what happened. Your rent payments become immediate costs of doing business; no depreciation to worry about. *The sum received from the sale is an immediate increment to capital.*

Here's how Richard E. Patzer, director of sales of Nationwide Development Company in Columbus, Ohio, explained it to me:

> Many people are only now becoming familiar with our activities in the field of leasebacks. Our present complex contains over forty leased properties, including offices, warehouses, financial institutions, department stores, supermarkets, convenience food stores, truck terminals, and drive-in restaurants. We also lease land on which two medical-professional buildings are located.
>
> Although there are virtually no limitations as to type of investment or prospect we are willing to consider, the following guidelines presently apply to our leaseback program:
>
> 1. Currently, in consideration of the present make-up of our investment portfolio, we are most interested in industrial facilities; freestanding commercial structures, involving businesses other than restaurant operations; transportation centers; distribution centers; or single-tenancy office buildings. This by no means rules out anything, but the types mentioned are most attractive to us.
>
> 2. We prefer leasebacks in the $250,000 to $1,000,000 range. However, we will consider those involving either lesser or greater amounts.
>
> 3. We currently seek a complete net return of 11 to 12 percent. This is return on total investment (for land and improvements) rather than return on equity, assuming existing mortgages or other financing is involved. This criteria is, of course, subject to re-evaluation and change. Each proposal is weighed on its individual merits.

4. In view of point 3 above, we realize that other than AAA-1 or large, long-established organizations may be involved. We will consider factors of location, type of facility concerned, company management, capitalization, and future business prospects. If small or fairly new firms are involved, we may also require additional security in the form of personal signatures, lease guarantee insurance, or the like.

5. We prefer a basic lease term of at least twenty years.

6. If a buy-back option is desired, we will consider including one, usually to be exercised only after the tenth year of the basic lease term and at a pre-established figure (usually not less than the amount of original investment, feeling land appreciation offsets building depreciation).

7. We pay full real estate commission.

8. Any proposed investment is subject to approval by our management and Board of Directors. With all necessary information at hand, a decision can usually be obtained within a matter of thirty days.

Before you sign any lease, whether for real property, cars, trucks, equipment, or whatever, you should find out certain things:

— Know the risks you are assuming.

— Assume as few risks as you can.

— Know whether the risks can be covered by insurance; is this your responsibility or that of the lessor?

8: Obvious but Unusual Avenues

Aﬁcionados of Conan Doyle's Sherlock Holmes—we're numbered in the millions—are familiar with Dr. John Watson's reactions to Holmes's *tours de force*. Initially astounded at his companion's complicated deductions, Watson inquires how it was done. "Oh, that," he exclaims after the explanation. "Anyone could have thought of it."

Money-raising suggestions in this chapter fall into such a Watsonian classification. Anyone could think of them. But most people don't.

Going Private

In an earlier chapter, experts delineated the differences between going public and going private. A coming chapter will delve into the mechanics, rationale, and advantages of going public. There's a lot to be said for going private, too.

Much of it was said in a March 7, 1971, article in the *New York Times* titled, appropriately, "Going Private."

106

"But, Poppa, the stock market's been going up for nine months. Let's try to take the company public again!"

That kind of thinking is growing these days and will probably grow some more in the wake of last week's bell-ringing public offering of Levi Strauss & Co., which went from $47 a share to $60 in less time than it takes to say "blue jeans."

But, says William M. Wolfson, owners of many other privately held companies might do just as well with another way of raising money: private placement of long-term debt.

Mr. Wolfson happens to be in charge of arranging private placements through Halle & Stieglitz, Inc., a brokerage and investment banking house of which he is senior vice president.

Despite this vested interest, Mr. Wolfson still thinks this is an excellent time for small-to-medium-sized companies to raise money through the private placement route.

A chief reason, he said, is that insurance companies, a prime market for private placements, have plenty of money to invest now, are less interested in the bond market than they were, and are willing to make "straight money" loans with no equity "kickers."

Other reasons he listed:

— Levi Strauss aside, the public's appetite for new equity issues has not reached the point where common stock underwritings can be a guaranteed success. Also, many owners of private companies may not want to worry about public shareholders.

— The time considerations involved in a public offering. Preparation of audits and registrations material for the Securities and Exchange Commission takes a minimum of four months, often more. Private placements usually can be arranged in a matter of weeks.

Mr. Wolfson said many insurance companies were interested in loans of $1 million to $3 million—the bigger companies prefer loans in the $10 million area—at interest rates of 8 to 9 percent. The minimum loan period usually is 10 years, and 15 years is preferred.

"It's amazing how many institutions are knocking on the door looking for loans of this sort," Mr. Wolfson said. "The insurance companies have a steady flow of money, and they have to put it somewhere. They're also finding that the drain on their funds from loans on policies is down sharply"—a result of the general decline in interest rates.

"We haven't seen a situation like this in years," Mr. Wolfson added, "and I don't think it's going to last too long." Money rates could go up again, he said, luring insurance company money back into bonds.

Factoring is used by many firms to raise money. The companies that furnish the money these days prefer the term "business financing" since it is both broader and more meaningful to clients than the more restrictive term "factoring."

Experts from the big firm of James Talcott, Inc., explained it in a question-and-answer brochure:

Q. *What is business financing?*
A. This . . . term . . . applies to loans . . . to commercial and industrial enterprises. These loans may be secured by . . . clients' inventories, machinery, fixed assets, accounts receivable, or other assets to provide the broadest possible borrowing base for both working capital and term loan requirements.

Q. *What is the basic purpose of business financing?*
A. As with most loans, business financing provides the funds necessary to promote the growth of a profitable or potentially profitable business. But with this difference business financing is usually sought when other primary sources of funds cannot or do not meet a firm's needs.

Q. *How and when can you use business financing?*
A. There are as many uses for financing as there are new horizons for profitable business. Here is just a partial list:

— To increase working capital during unusual periods of growth to avoid a cash shortage. Or to maintain a supply of readily available capital at a constant level.

— To obtain funds during business readjustment periods when financing is not available in sufficient quantity from banks . . . or when equity or institutional financing is not feasible.

— To pay or discount trade bills. Often the discounts earned in this manner can offset the cost of financing.

— To modernize, replace, or automate equipment and facilities.

— To refinance present debt.

— To carry on highly seasonal activities that require a large pre-season inventory . . . and which will show post-seasonal peaks in receivables.

— To finance mergers or the acquisition of other businesses, . . . to buy out partnership interests, . . . to purchase a business from trustees of estates, . . . to provide the wherewithal to accomplish sound reorganizations.

— To purchase a new plant or equipment—or for any "capital loan" purpose.

— To finance imports through letters of credit.

Q. How does business financing work?

A. . . . We will mutually determine the size and type of loan your business requires to achieve its goals. Then Talcott surveys your business and considers every aspect of it—from your product, to plant and equipment, to marketing and sales, to your future prospects—and more. Our purpose is to establish the broadest possible borrowing base for your firm so that your present and future needs can be met and any or all of your company and its operations may form the basis for collateral.

Q. Who can use business financing?

A. Almost every type of manufacturing or distributing organization may someday find business financing a valuable and necessary tool that can substantially further its corporate growth. From automotive parts to zippers, . . . manufacturers of both metal or plastic products, machinery, electronics or soft goods, . . . from small consumer products to massive industrial manufacturers, . . . all types of food processors, . . . distributors and dealers, . . . printers, advertising firms, and other organizations—all these and more have found financing an important assist when needed.

Q. What are the usual results of business financing for the company using it?

A. Our experience has shown that most client companies increase their sales and profits substantially. You will find that as you generate new volume, you simultaneously create a broader borrowing base. Thus, you have a flexible, revolving fund of credit—which grows with your needs—available to you for immediate use.

Q. How fast can financing be provided?

A. Generally within several days. . . . The initial loan is made immediately after simple contractual arrangements are completed. Thereafter, new or continuing loans are made as rapidly as funds can be transferred by wire to your bank— usually within an hour or two.

Q. Is commercial financing competitive with unsecured bank financing?

A. No. It is a supplemental or complementary means of financing.

Q. What does this service cost?

A. Charges for this service are more reasonable than you may think. There is a single fraction of a percentage point charged on the daily loan balance due from your company. The charge is calculated each month end for that month. The charge is dependent on the size of the loan, quality, and work involved. Unlike a bank loan, charges are not discounted in advance. The service works on an availability of funds fixed to an agreed ratio of collateral. You can draw funds from this "availability" as your business needs arise. Thus you control the loan balance in use from day to day and can minimize or maximize your usage and costs.

Q. What other considerations should a businessman study when thinking of using business financing?

A. First, you should investigate the reputation, experience, resources, and knowledgeability of the finance organization you are considering. Then ask yourself what the funds derived from this financing technique will do for your company. If this is the logical way your company can borrow the funds needed to properly conduct its business—can you afford not to borrow, considering the broadened profit opportunity these extra dollars may represent?

Q. Is business financing right for all businesses?

A. No. If your company has plenty of working capital and is able to borrow from a bank on an unsecured basis enough to handle peak requirements easily—then business financing arrangements offer no advantage for you.

Q. How large or small does a business have to be to benefit from business financing?

A. Financing has been extended to thousands of companies whose annual sales range from a low of $500,000 to those with sales well in excess of $100 million yearly. Such a range demonstrates the almost universal application and usefulness of this popular financing technique. Of course, vigorous young businesses with growing sales which would ordinarily not seem to qualify on a minimal basis will be welcomed if other indications are encouraging.

Q. Will the use of business financing impair your company's trade credit standing?

A. On the contrary, it usually improves your company's credit standing. When your company borrows against its collateral, it is cashing its approximate cost of sales. This makes it possible for the company to buy more goods, pay its trade debts and other obligations promptly, and profitably expand its production and sales. Knowledgeable trade credit executives recommend that their customers use this type of financing. They realize that companies eligible for business finance credit lines are apt to be growing companies on their way up to leadership in their respective industries.

Q. How do business financing and factoring differ?

A. Business financing makes use of your assets—whether inventory, plant and equipment, real estate, or receivables— but only as collateral. On the other hand, broadly speaking, in a factoring arrangement, your receivables are purchased outright, and the factor becomes your credit department and collects billings directly from your customers.

Borrow on Insurance

Insurance companies have furnished "going private" funds for many businesses. They also furnish money to a different kind of borrower, often one starting a business for the first time, and they do not always do this willingly. The reason is that the interest rate charges are in many cases far below going interest rates. That's bad for the lender, but good for you if you choose this avenue for raising funds.

Sometimes it can be used for only minor (but frequently needed) amounts of money. Other times the amounts are substantial. In a May 24, 1969, article in *Business Week*, during an historically high period for interest percentages, the workings of this method were explained:

> Grey Advertising, Inc., asked for and got a loan of more than a half-million dollars at 5 percent simple interest during the past year while plenty of other companies literally went begging for money at 10 percent, 12 percent, 14 percent, and more.
>
> Grey doesn't necessarily have special pull with its lender. In fact, practically any company—or an individual for that matter —could tap a similar source. Grey simply borrowed the cash values from life insurance policies carried on key officers. The loan, amounting to more than 20 percent of its cash flow in 1968, helped Grey to build up working capital and hold down expensive bank borrowings.
>
> Because policy loan rates are fixed at 5 percent or 6 percent while other borrowing rates are not, the volume of such insurance loans has soared. Loans as a percent of life reserves of insurance companies jumped to 11.2 percent in 1966 from the 9.9 percent of 1965 that had been about the average for years. Last year the figure was 12.5 percent and signs are the volume for 1969 will be higher yet—13 percent or more.
>
> And with the average return on life insurers' investments running between 5 percent and 5½ percent, the companies should be as happy making loans as the policyholders are to get them. But this is hardly the case.
>
> Making the loan is not an investment decision on the company's part—it's an obligation. Not only is there no control over timing, policy loans never have to be repaid.

Policyholders who borrow are simply getting back their own savings that have built up through level premium payments on whole life policies. This kind of coverage is by far the most heavily sold kind of ordinary life insurance. In effect, the policyholder builds his own death benefit fund; the company manages its investment and assures the policyholder that, if he dies before his accumulated savings equal the policy's face value, the company will pay the difference.

Property You Already Own

If you own your home, have purchased a lot in Arizona or Florida for later retirement—not one of the flaky pieces of real estate peddled so often on which regulators have pounced so hard—or other mortgagable property, you have a source of borrowed capital. This is true even where it's already covered by mortgage. In many cases, payments that have been made have increased your equity and therefore ability to borrow. Sometimes, appreciation of the property gives a base for additional borrowing.

You've got to understand what you are doing, of course. You are risking the very roof over your family's head. It's better, therefore, not to go too deeply into this method of financing without having thought things out with great care and having examined the possibilities for losing out as well as winning in that new business venture.

If you decide to go ahead, as a cost-control measure it is well to know about the newest wrinkle. This is called a variable-rate mortgage. The Federal Reserve Bank of San Francisco described it in its *Monthly Review* of April 1972:

As the term implies, a variable-rate mortgage (VRM) differs from the standard fixed-rate mortgage in that the contract interest rate may vary over the life of the loan. A VRM may assume either of two forms, although both entail changes in the interest component of the amortized loan.

The first type of VRM adjusts the monthly payment to reflect a change in the interest rate, with the maturity of the loan remaining the same. Consider a new $20,000.00 mortgage loan with a 25-year maturity and an initial contract interest rate of 8 percent. The monthly payment (interest and principal) on such a loan would amount to $154.40. But if, at the end of one year, the rate of interest fell to 7.5 percent in response to a decline in other interest rates, the new monthly payment would be set at a level that would pay off the loan balance ($19,737.80) over the remaining 24 years of the loan. The new monthly payment thereupon would fall to $147.98 from the original $154.40. A raise in interest rates of course would mean a higher rather than a lower monthly payment.

The second type of VRM adjusts the maturity of the loan to reflect a change in the interest rate, with the monthly payment left unchanged. In the above example, a constant monthly payment, combined with a drop in the interest rate from 8 to 7.5 percent after one year, would be sufficient to pay off the loan in 21 years and 6 months rather than the original 24 years. But, here again, a rise in interest rates would mean a longer rather than a shorter loan maturity.

A variable-rate mortgage essentially is an escalator-type agreement of the type widely used throughout the economy—in cost-of-living adjustments to wage and pension agreements, in rental-property contracts (especially for office buildings), and in welfare and alimony payments. (Many escalator agreements provide only for upward movement, however, while the VRM would provide for movement in both directions.) Commercial banks sometimes include escalator clauses in the loan agreements they make with business borrowers, and for that matter, the Home Loan Banks frequently attach escalator clauses to the advances they make to savings-and-loan associations. . . .

In actuality, the variable-rate mortgage has received only limited acceptance in this country. A 1969 survey by the U.S. Savings and Loan League revealed that only 10 percent of its surveyed members had rate-adjustment clauses in their loan contracts, and no more than an additional 10 percent planned to employ them in the future. A majority of those associations that actually used VRMs applied them to less than 20 percent of their loans, and a substantial part of these were commercial rather than residential mortgages.

A 1970 survey by the American Bankers Association showed that 18 percent of the surveyed banks utilized VRMs and in these, too, their use was limited primarily to commercial properties. (VRMs were used in the financing of single-family housing in only five states—four of them in New England.) Again, half of those banks that actually used VRMs employed them in less than 1 percent of the mortgage loans they originated in 1969. In the West, commercial banks have utilized variable-rate loans only to a limited extent, while only a half dozen or so S&Ls have actively written such loans. Apparently, the difficulty of reconciling the differing interests of borrowers and lenders has tended to limit its more widespread acceptance.

If you're negotiating a mortgage in low-interest times, forget the VRM. It is to your advantage then to string out the terms at the going rate. But if you're working on a loan when money is tight and costly to rent (interest is nothing more than a rental charge on money), then remember the variable rate mortgage and try your best to get one.

Will the State or County Furnish Funds?

After World War II, energetic Mississippians looked at their state. It was in a cotton economy reminiscent of post-Civil War days. Industries were small, few, and often primitive. Having had a taste during World War II of what industrial payrolls can do for a region's prosperity, Mississippians inaugurated something that they called Balance Agriculture With Industry. It was usually referred to as BAWI. Within a dozen years, BAWI transformed the state. At first small industries came in. Then larger ones.

The core of the BAWI idea was that a community could sell bonds, build a plant to order for a company that contemplated using it, and contract for the company to rent the plant, paying for its eventual ownership out of the rentals. You risked nothing to start such a business in Mississippi.

The idea has been both criticized and praised since. Most important, it has been widely copied in one form or another.

Therefore, it can pay to determine whether your area has something similar to BAWI—under whatever name—and whether it applies to the business you plan to start. If so, financing can be arranged in many cases in a single package.

A Commercial Finance Company

Individuals in need of money (usually at high cost) can turn to Friendly Sam or Cheerful Freddy, the stock character at the corner finance office where, for interest rates as high as 50 percent a year, they can obtain loans. A commercial finance company is something like that, but you won't pay rates up to 50 percent. How much you will pay often depends upon your negotiating ability.

Aetna Business Credit, Inc., a subsidiary of Aetna Insurance, described the diversity and availability of financing through such a firm:

> Following is a list of established borrowing methods around which a package plan can be designed. Business Credit is not limited to these methods. Using creative financing techniques such as combining assets, we often design alternative plans to meet special situations.

> *Accounts Receivable*
> Accounts receivable can be pledged as collateral for loans. Typically an 80 percent advance is made against eligible accounts. The assignment is handled on a non-notification revolving basis and is self-liquidating. Interest charges are billed on the basis of actual daily cash loan balances. This monthly charge is frequently less than missed cash discounts.

> *Factoring*
> Factoring is the outright sale of trade accounts on a non-

recourse basis. Factoring enables a business to eliminate a credit and collection department as well as losses due to bad debts. Aetna Business Credit, as factor, will buy outright all accounts receivable approved by it at a nominal discount. This enables the client to concentrate on production, purchasing, and sell-ing—the profit tools of any business.

Inventory Loans

Inventory loans are available to accounts receivable and factor-ing clients. Such loans are frequently utilized to assist the custo-mer during periods of slow product shipments and inventory build-up or to facilitate bulk raw material purchases at advan-tageous prices.

Capital Loans

Aetna Business Credit will make capital loans on plant ma-chinery and equipment. These advances are normally amor-tized monthly over a period of one to five years . . . or even more. The proceeds from this type of loan may be required by the borrower to increase working capital, discount accounts payable, or simply to purchase new equipment. Very often an equipment loan is accepted in conjunction with accounts receivable or factoring arrangements.

Time Sales Financing

Aetna Business Credit provides funds to manufacturers and distributors on time sales paper arising from the sale of income-producing equipment. Flexibility permits a wide latitude in the selection of maturities, down payments, amortization sched-ules, as well as rates and recourse provisions.

Equipment Leasing

Aetna Business Credit is able to handle any equipment leasing requirements that may arise: either by acting as lessor or through established leasing companies with which it has a working relationship.

A complete selection of plans is available to provide the lessee with satisfactory terms as to advance rentals, lease term, purchase options, and rental rates.

Re-Discounting

Aetna Business Credit's resources allow it to act as a source of working capital to firms holding portfolios of open accounts or installment sales. Bulk purchases of such receivables can provide funds to establish new outstandings or for other business purposes.

Medium-sized finance companies that cannot obtain sufficient bank credit find that re-discounting enables them to obtain adequate funds for continued growth.

Real Estate Financing

For many years, Aetna Business Credit has provided cash for first and junior mortgages on income producing commercial and residential buildings as well as industrial and other real properties.

Export-Import Financing

Aetna Business Credit can assist the international transactions of clients with letters of credit and advise on documentation, export credit insurance, and foreign exchange. It has close connections with the international financing community.

Special Situation Financing

If a merger, acquisition, buy-out, or any other credit-worthy transaction doesn't fit established borrowing methods, Aetna Business Credit has the people, know-how, and funds to build a loan around a client's special requirements. This is flexible financing in action.

Personal Credit

You probably have personal credit availability you don't even know about, above and beyond the bank, the SBA, and all the others. You see the ads for these firms regularly in financial journals. They are addressed to "executives," which is a rather elastic term covering a very elastic class. The ads promise confidentiality and promptness. I sent for material to several of these sources to examine for purposes of this book.

One of them wrote to me:

For years, executive and professional men have lived with the problem of not being able to get large, unsecured loans in strict confidence. I feel that we've solved the problem by combining privacy, reliability, and convenience in a fast loan-by-mail service. Here are the details in a nutshell.

We assure your privacy by doing business through the mail only. We make no inquiries of your business associates, your friends, or your neighbors. What's more, our envelopes and checks are designed to maintain the privacy of your loan. Our mail to you will never be any less discreet than this letter.

And we require no personal interviews or long questionnaires. We don't even ask why you want the loan, so what you do with it is as confidential as the loan itself.

The enclosed payment schedule is proof that we don't charge you for this privacy. To the best of our knowledge, our annual percentage rate of 16 percent is more favorable to you than the rates offered by any similar service anywhere in the country. This, combined with the fact that we lend up to $10,000 and offer a wide range of maturities, makes our service especially attractive.

I am not personally as convinced as was the writer of this letter that 16 percent is any kind of "favorable" rate. But these companies are a source of funds worth knowing about. All specialize in loans by mail. A list includes:

Dial Finance Corporation, Executive and Professional Loan Division, 418 Seventh St., Des Moines, Iowa 50309.

Security Financial, 4630 Geary Blvd., San Francisco, California 94118.

Carter Shields, Inc., P.O. Box 509, Shawano, Wisconsin 54166.

Easier to use, but still expensive, is your BankAmericard or Master Charge account. If you have, for example, an upper limit of $1,000 on regular credit, you can obtain this amount in supplies or equipment ($2,000 if you use both BankAmericard and Master Charge). You'll be required to pay back only a small amount each month, but will be hit with a big 18 percent a year (smaller percentages in a few states) for the privileges of using this handy but expensive credit.

However, you can utilize both Master Charge and Bank-Americard *entirely without interest cost* if you do it this way:

1. Determine the billing date of your account. This is different for each customer. Say, for example, that yours is the eighteenth of the month.

2. On the nineteenth, rush out and buy supply or equipment needs for your new business, which can be purchased on the credit card.

3. You now have not thirty but fifty-five days to pay. The reason is that you can stretch things not only over the normal month, but twenty-five days beyond—on most Bank-Americard or Master Charge plans since these have slight differences from sponsoring bank to sponsoring bank—without interest cost.

Another (and odd) source of money for a new business is from a Loans to Heirs company. If you have an inheritance that is currently going through probate, or an estate left in trust on which you cannot employ principal but only receive the regular income, Allied Investment and Discount Corp., 1530 Locust Street, Philadelphia, Pennsylvania 19102, will discuss a cash-now arrangement with you, using the estate as collateral.

9: Going Public

P_{AST} chapters have considered the advantages and disadvantages, the wheels, ways, whys, and wherefores, of largely private means of raising capital. Common to all of these methods is that the company and its control stay in the hands of those who started it and nursed it—as long as they continue to pay the notes due.

This chapter looks into how to go public, a subject discussed briefly earlier in the book.

Common to the methods of going public is the fact that the owners are no longer able to wheel and deal as they please, and in some circumstances, although they may remain as the titular bosses, they have to take into account the wishes and needs of a host of new owners. It may be a wrench to do so, but the pain is lessened when you look at all the dollars raised without any need to pay them back. Going public involves watering the ownership, but the money obtained from it stays in the business.

(Going public is a technique more applicable to an existing business that the owners wish to expand than to a totally new firm that, at the time of money-raising, is no more than a gleam in the entrepreneur's eye, a design on a clipboard, and a set of accountant's projected figures. But going public *can* be applied—and has been—in raising funds for a scratch-new business.)

Going public looks easy, but it is not. Some once-eager stock sellers have found that going public is not just a matter of eager investors shoving cash into their coffers. It involves some formidable headaches. Yet others say that going public is the only way to grow. Let's look at the question from both sides.

Many small businesses start with capital supplied by the owners and their friends, with perhaps a sizable chunk from rich old Uncle George. That kind of financing is fine as long as it lasts. But if the company is ably managed and succeeds, its owners will want to expand. In this day of high taxes, few companies can generate internally the kind of cash they need for expansion. They can borrow, but borrowing power is sometimes slight while the assets available for collateral are small, and managements tend to find that banks are unwilling to tie up long-term money.

Long ago, the great Samuel Johnson presided at the sale of a brewery. "We are not here to sell vats and boilers," he said, "but to grow rich beyond the dreams of avarice." If you go public and if your company succeeds, and if you catch Wall Street's fickle fancy, and if you avoid a thousand extra regulatory reefs and sandbars, and if you have the right underwriter, and if a couple of hundred other things all come out right, then you can indeed grow rich by going public— perhaps even beyond the dreams of avarice. It is happening right now.

Consider these pro and con angles to going public:

Pro: You change your company from a personal possession into an

*organization that is able to outlast you and to generate income for
your family after you have gone.*

It has been the fate of many private entrepreneurs that the
organizations they built died with them or had to be peddled
at bargain basement prices by their survivors. In another,
simpler day a son succeeded his father in the family's business. But no more. Sons and sons-in-law follow other profes-
sions, often far afield and frequently far removed geographi-
cally. So it is a problem to leave something financially meaningful to your family.

Public ownership avoids the necessity of liquidation for
taxes. It is able to attract a professional management group
and such a group, by its nature, attracts and names its succes-
sors so that service to the public survives. And the original
owner's survivors benefit.

Pro: Going public establishes a value for personal holdings.
"Until we went public, I had a big chunk of ownership in
some land, a few buildings, and the profits of a going organization," one executive reported when asked why his company sold stock to investors. "But what was I worth? How can
anyone establish a valuation of land and the buildings that
are ideal for one specialized purpose but perhaps useless for
any other? My share of profits was worth—what?

"Now I have a measurement of personal worth. I can say
to the tax collector, to my accountant, to my banker if I want
a loan, that I have holdings of x-many dollars, not of bricks
and mortar. There is no way to establish what the stock you
hold is worth until you sell some of it and a public market is
developed."

Pro: A publicly owned corporation can attract better executives.
Stock options allow a manager to build his estate and to pay
taxes on a capital gains basis. Stock options depend on a liquid
public market, which sets the value of the stock executives
buy (usually at a discount) and which will furnish a valuation
as well as a possible place to sell when a manager later

decides to cash his option stocks. Options roughly relate pay to performance since profit growth of a company is usually rewarded by higher stock prices. And stock options are a fine way to compensate yourself, too.

Pro: You can arrange quick personal loans if they are needed. Emergencies that require sudden large amounts of cash arise in every family. Most of us borrow from a bank when that happens. Banks lend the biggest percentage of collateral, usually at the lowest personal interest rates, on stocks if these are publicly traded.

Pro: The stock is available for further financing. Common stock, warrants convertible into stock at their holders' option, and preferred stock or debentures also convertible into common are the usual currency of expansion moves. All of these require a public market as base.

You may not want to expand further now, but some time in the future, opportunity or need may make you wish you had the currency to expand into an allied field. Going public can build the base for later moves.

Con: Disclosure, disclosure, disclosure. "Before you get finished with registration," confided one man whose company recently went public, "you will be disclosing your brand of toothpaste and whether the drug store at which you buy it is run by a relative or close friend."

Things aren't really that bad. But men who thought that their business affairs were their own or, at worst, a confidential matter between themselves and the tax collector, have discovered that there is nothing about business operations that remains private after plans jell to sell stock to investors. This is, of course, the way things should be, for after a company goes public its corporate comings and goings are no longer the private affair of one or a few men. There are new owners. These people have a right to know what the bosses once kept to themselves.

But it is not always pleasant to live in a goldfish bowl. Among other drawbacks to the regulatory aspect is the fact that every time you buy and sell what you once regarded as *your* firm's stock, you will have to report the transaction to the Securities and Exchange Commission. Depending upon laws of your state, you may have to make another disclosure to state officials. Certain kinds of trading in your own stock will be prohibited. You can even be sued for triple damages on prohibited kinds of capital gain transactions in your stock. In certain circumstances, you might be prosecuted criminally for utilizing what is called inside information before the public has been given time not only to receive but also to assimilate any fresh developments.

Con: It costs a great deal to go through registration. Firms that relied on local legal talent to handle their affairs have found that, after going public, this is not always enough. Often a Washington lawyer has to be kept on retainer, and the cost of steering things through regulatory mazes can sometimes become sizable.

I recently read the file on registration (a public document) of one company that went public. There were forty-two revisions and changes to the registration statement. Each of these consumed the time of expensive legal experts.

To that expense you can add the cost of separate registration in most states in which stock will be sold. It is true that these chores are often handled by the legal staffs of investment bankers who underwrite new issues. But they cost money regardless of whose lawyers do them and hence must show up in the bill for going public.

Con: It takes a long time to go public. The forty-two revisions mentioned above consumed nearly a year. Often an expansion opportunity that could have been seized and exploited at the right time slips away by the time such a lengthy process happens. "You might go broke waiting," warns one investment banker. "Therefore, don't depend upon the proceeds of going public for any funds you might need in a hurry."

Con: There will be continuing cost of added records. A company that belongs to outsiders has to keep many more records than the simple ones needed by a privately or closely held entity.

There are added bank fees to pay. Stocks trade back and forth, and every time they change hands they must be transferred anew and put into the names of new owners. Most firms arrange with banks to handle this and so escape the paperwork blizzard. But the banks do not perform for free, and their fees can add up to considerable amounts.

Con: Public relations problems become more acute. Most companies deal with only two publics. One is the public of the customer. The other is the public of the community in which a firm operates and with which it must maintain good relations and a good image. When that firm sells stock to outsiders, there suddenly enters a wholly new public in the form of stockholders and the financial community.

Financial public relations constitute a world of their own. A man or firm adept at communicating with families, neighbors, and the general public does not always succeed in arranging the right kind of image with mutual funds and banks, with the financial analysts whose recommendations sometimes set a stock plummeting or shooting toward the top of the chart, and with that most delicate public of all, the people who hold certificates making them part owners of the company. Unhappily, there are not many people skilled in this sort of public relations, and their services do not come cheap.

Con: Where will Wall Street's fancy light tomorrow? In 1960 the chemical stocks were public darlings. In 1961 it was the far-out little science firms. 1962 was a bear year; nothing was hot. In 1963 and 1964 the staid blue chips were the apples of Wall Streeters' eyes. Then in 1965 small research and development stocks had the play, along with airlines. 1966 saw another down market. But 1967 was a good year for "conceptual" stocks with a story fitting into new social conditions. In 1968 it was the franchisers, and 1969—generally a down year—found nursing homes in favor.

But what will go up next? A fact of life to be considered in the decision to go public is the fickleness of Wall Street's fads and booms.

Con: You can lose your business to a corporate raider. Unless blocks of stock large enough to add up to majority control are in the hands of known friends, the risk is always there that if you succeed, some acquisition-minded company might come along with a tender offer, and suddenly you are no longer the owner of what was once your own company.

To these pro and con considerations there is no right answer. No one can say that going public is good or bad per se. But there is a right answer for an individual entrepreneur considering the question. Careful weighing of the factors set forth may help him arrive at that correct decision.

Letter Stock

There are three easier ways to go public. One is issuance of what is called *letter stock* or *restricted securities*.

Publicly sold stocks and other securities have to go through registration. If sold inside a state, they must usually be registered with state authorities. If sold interstate, they must be registered with the Securities and Exchange Commission.

Letter stock lets you avoid—or postpone—all of this. Say you negotiate with a mutual fund to sell 100,000 shares of letter stock. Public stock might be trading at 20. The fund manager is likely to offer you from 13 to 15 for the stock. He will say, "Ah, yes, there is a discount. But it may be no bigger than the cost of registering and selling an issue to the public. With us, you get the proceeds now. No waiting. That means inflation won't have eaten up part of the value of the funds before they reach your hands."

You may or may not agree with the fund man's reasoning. If you should agree, he will extract a stipulation to go through registration later so the stock can be sold. Meanwhile, he will hold the stock on a letter of intent stating that it was purchased for long-term investment and not for distribution through public channels.

A "Regulation A" Offering

"Reg A" is the second way to simplify the going public process. It won't make things as easy as issuance of letter stock, but you'll find it simpler in most cases to go Reg A than to find a mutual fund or other institution willing to accept and pay for letter stock—especially if your firm is new and untried.

Writing in the *New England Business Review* of the Federal Reserve Bank of Boston, Daniel Ounjian of Tufts University noted:

> Under this regulation, firms issuing securities in amounts of $300,000 [now $500,000] or less are exempt from the more stringent—and expensive—SEC registration procedures required of other public issues. Relatively simple "letters of notification" and much less detailed offering circulars—both designed so that average businessmen can complete them without professional help—replace complex prospectuses and certified financial statements.
>
> Regulation A thus offers many small businessmen an opportunity to enter the capital funds market on essentially their own terms . . . or more accurately, perhaps, on terms less prohibitive in time, sophistication, and money than would otherwise be possible. But it provides somewhat less reliable information for the protection of potential investors. . . .
>
> This study of how the Reg A market operates was based on a random sample of 125 filings, which after eliminating withdrawals, secondary issues, etc., left 78 security issues offered publicly for cash in 1959. The year was deliberately selected to reflect a time when conditions appeared favorable for attempts to raise funds on the public market. Also, the time elapsed was long enough to observe the sales success of the offerings and permit some evaluation of the performance of the issuing companies.
>
> One dominant characteristic of the sampled issuers was the youth of the firms. Two-thirds were less than five years old, and 36 percent had been incorporated for less than a full year at the time of the offering. For the vast majority this was the first attempt at a public offering.

The industrial composition of the issuers varies from year to year depending on prevailing fads. . . . Of the sampled firms, about one-third were in manufacturing, with almost half of that number in electronics. Another third were in miscellaneous commercial businesses—particularly discount stores and such leisure enterprises as vacation resorts and boat companies. . . .

Although a few issuers had assets of over $1 million, most had considerably less. More than three-quarters had assets of less than half a million dollars; 37 percent had assets of less than $100,000. In terms of owners' equity, the figures were even lower, with the median at $80,000.

The typical offering was common stock with expected proceeds of about $250,000. Roughly one-third of the sampled issues were of the maximum size. About 15 percent of the offerings were debt, preferred, and combination issues, and these were from older, relatively large companies with more equity.

In general, the offerings were of sizable proportions relative to the existing scale of operations, thus reflecting the importance of the issue for corporate expansion. Out of seventy-eight sampled issues, 60 percent were successfully marketed either by promoters or underwriters, with success defined as the sale of at least 85 percent of the proposed dollar offering. Of the successful issues, more than one-half were completed within two months from the initial date of the offering. Although ten issuers achieved success in six months or longer, the probabilities of being so fortunate diminish as time passes. The study data suggest that the chances of floating successful issues would improve if those that were not selling rapidly were withdrawn after a few months and new offerings made at a later, more opportune time. Like most merchandise, a security offering can become "shopworn," and even a subsequent market boom can be of little help. . . .

A factor related to successful marketing was found to be commercial underwriting. Underwriting agreements in the small issues market are almost always on a "best efforts" basis; that is, the underwriter agrees to do his best to sell the issue but, failing to do so, is not obligated to buy the unsold securities. Although this method offers no guarantee of success, more than twice as many commercially underwritten issues were successfully marketed as those offered directly by promoters or officers of the issuers. Furthermore, commercial underwriters sold on the average 90 percent of the amount of each issue initially offered, while direct promoters succeeded in selling only 50 percent. Thus, the existence of an organized distributing mechanism seemed related to the successful distribution of Reg A issues.

It seems logical to assume that at least part of the apparent sales success of the underwriters might be traced to their marketing abilities. They, almost by definition, would have access to a wider potential market for small blocks of these speculative shares—and, by knowing their customers' inclinations, might be expected to place the issues more efficiently and effectively.

Because of their knowledge of the market and its requirements, the underwriters, in many cases, were in a position to advise the issuers they served on such helpful matters as pricing and promotion, which increase the market's interest in the stock offered. . . .

Selecting the underwriter is perhaps one of the most difficult decisions the issuer must make. For the most part, the larger established investment houses rarely concern themselves with small issues, and with the possible exception of favors for friends, Reg A issues are the domain of marginal firms. Typically, these firms enter the industry only after a boom has gotten under way and retreat the moment it shows signs of subsiding. . . .

"Shopping around" for the best deal is not recommended. Without assurance of getting the issue, underwriters are generally unwilling to incur the expenses of investigation. They would lose interest quickly if word were to circulate that a company was negotiating with two or more firms simultaneously. Altogether, local contacts and coincidence—more than carefully planned selection—appear to account for the choices made by many issuers. . . .

The knottiest problems in the negotiations between an issuer and underwriter are the establishment of an offering price, the amount of the offering, the number of shares to be sold, and the underwriter's fee. Generally, the public offering price is based on a number of factors, the most important being the market price of essentially the same type of securities. For young unknown companies, however, the most important considerations center on a realistic appraisal of market conditions and especially on investors' attitudes toward securities of new small companies.

Flotation costs of the sampled offerings ranged widely and varied with the type of securities and the method of offering. For commercially underwritten common stock, of every dollar collected from the public, an average of 16.5 cents went to pay underwriters, lawyers, accountants, printers, taxes, and other expenses. Flotation costs for directly offered issues were somewhat less.

In addition to their commissions, underwriters often insist on and obtain options to buy large blocks of shares in the issuing corporation. In more than half of the sampled underwritten offerings, investment bankers had procured options, frequently at prices substantially below the issue price. Such practices may open the door to the possibility of financial manipulation and abuses. . . .

In an attempt to discover how the sampled firms had fared in the years following their issue of stock . . . data from Dun and Bradstreet and the National Quotation Bureau were analyzed. Although no trace could be found of fourteen sampled issuers in these sources, some information was available on the other sixty-four firms. . . . Sixty firms were still operating either independently, as parts of new firms resulting from mergers, or as subsidiaries. Of the other four, Dun and Bradstreet reported that one could not be found, one had its offering suspended by the SEC and never started its business, and two went bankrupt. Detailed operating data were available for fifty-two firms, and about two-thirds of them were showing rising sales.

A "Shell"

The third short-cut to going public is fraught with peril. It has been used so many times by so many shady characters as a way of distributing stock to the public without complying with laws and regulations, and has been the tool employed in so many cases to manipulate and fake stock prices and values, that the Securities and Exchange Commission and many state regulators look with jaundiced eyes on many shell corporations. Yet they can be useful. You'd better be very careful before going this route.

From time to time, there are ads in financial publications offering shell corporations. Typical was one in the *Wall Street Journal* of February 16, 1971. It was headlined: "Investment Banking Firm Has Available For Merger Two Publicly Held Shell Companies Trading OTC."

Shells are corporations that have gone out of business, leaving only a shell that may or may not have the following assets: cash, or something such as Treasury bills, notes, or bonds that are equivalent to cash; real estate; a building or two; a mining claim (usually either played out or originally devoid of value— many shells were once uranium mining companies); and, most important, stock for which there is still a market, however small.

Someone acquiring a shell corporation can use the stock to buy up other assets (e.g., a business he wants to start), and the company can be used as a vehicle for issuance of debentures, etc.

The truth about the usually worthless securities of a shell must be told the public at all times. To give insight into the danger (and opportunities) of a shell, there is release number 8724 from the Securities and Exchange Commission:

> The Securities and Exchange Commission today ordered the temporary suspension under the Securities Exchange Act of 1934 of over-the-counter trading in the securities of Ocean Data Industries, Inc., formerly Lisbon Valley Uranium, of 1615 North Atlantic Avenue, Cocoa Beach, Florida, for the ten-day period October 21, 1969, through October 30, 1969. Trading in Ocean Data Industries may resume October 31, 1969.
>
> The Commission announced it took this action because of the

lack of adequate or accurate information available concerning Ocean Data Industries, Inc., its operations, or financial condition. Inquiry by the staff of the Commission has disclosed that there may be inaccuracies in information disseminated by Ocean Data Industries. The Commission cautioned investors and broker-dealers to consider the facts set forth in a letter the company has recently sent to shareholders.

The Commission cautions broker-dealers to consider their responsibilities under the securities laws for full disclosure of all material facts in connection with the execution of security transactions and again directs the attention of the brokerage community and the investing public to Securities Act Release No. 4982, dated July 2, 1969, entitled "Application of the Securities Act of 1933 and the Securities Exchange Act of 1934 to Spin-Offs in Securities and Trading in the Securities of Inactive or Shell Corporations," and Securities Act Release No. 4445, dated February 2, 1962, entitled "Distribution by Broker-Dealers of Unregistered Securities."

The Securities Act registration requirements are designed to provide disclosure of financial and other information about the issuer and its securities to enable investors to make an informed and realistic evaluation of the securities. Failure to comply with the registration requirements may deprive investors of much or all of this essential information and the protection that the Securities Act seeks to provide. The absence of such information facilitates false claims as to the worth of the securities.

The Commission advises that utmost care should be exercised by brokers and dealers, stockholders, and prospective stockholders in reading and analyzing this release and any other information available about this company.

Because of the above and the information contained in the shareholder letter recently sent to stockholders . . . the Commission cautions broker-dealers that before effecting transactions in the securities of Ocean Data Industries, Inc., they have the obligation of assuring themselves that such transactions are in compliance with the registration and other applicable provisions of the federal securities laws. Moreover, broker-dealers who solicit the purchase of the securities of Ocean Data Industries, Inc., without first making diligent inquiry to determine all pertinent financial and other information about the issuer and disclosing such information to prospective purchasers, may be engaging in violations of the anti-fraud provisions of the federal securities laws. In addition, brokers and dealers who publish quotations and trade in this company's securities should assure themselves that they are not participating in activities that make them participants in violation of the registration provisions of the Securities Act or the anti-fraud and anti-manipulative provisions of the Securities Act and the Securities Exchange Act. The Commission also stated it was continuing its investigation in this matter.

Mergers and Acquisitions

You can finance a going (but not a new) business by means of merger. You receive stock of a publicly traded company, which in turn acquires your operation. The company receives access to the larger treasury of its merger partner, thus financing expansion. It isn't too usual a route for young companies—most going public methods apply to the going, existing concern—but should be understood by every entrepreneur seeking capital.

In every financial center there are merger-acquisition firms —often listed under that heading, or under "financial advisory," or even misleadingly under "investment advisory." If you're interested in being merged or acquired, search out one of these middlemen. They're on the lookout for candidates. Most receive finders' fees from big companies for unearthing interesting small situations.

Sometimes banks act as middlemen. The Northern Trust Company of Chicago noted in a booklet describing its merger acquisition service:

> Finding suitable acquisition candidates is our most important work for buyers. We are uniquely set up to do this.
> A communication network that is national and international in scope brings many substantial companies to our offices.

Our commercial banking and trust officers in their customer, prospect, and industry contacts are constantly on the alert for those who are considering sale.

In addition, domestic and foreign correspondent banks, investment bankers, attorneys, business brokers, management consultants, and accountants are all valuable sources of buying opportunities for us.

We make sure that each of our referrals has been carefully considered and has relevance for the buyer. Ours is the "rifle" rather than the "shotgun" approach.

Our services for buyers include:

— *Gathering data on potential sellers*, such as ownership, financial statements, reputation, principal bank, willingness to talk, etc.

— *Bringing parties together* on neutral ground.

— *Assisting in negotiations*, suggesting terms, providing creative financing programs and technical assistance.

— *Evaluating a selling company's worth*, as well as a buying company's diversification plan.

— *Providing complete commercial banking and trust services*, ranging from developing sources of funds to serving as trustee on a debenture issue.

Many compelling reasons can lead the owners or managers of a company to a decision to sell all or a part of the enterprise. Legitimate business and personal goals can be realized by doing so.

For example, a medium-sized growth company might keep its competitive edge and, in fact, grow faster by merging with a company that has the required resources—whether they take the form of ample capital or strong international capabilities.

Whatever the reasons—the liquidation of an estate, the onrush of competition, or the need for new products or new capital—merger or acquisition may be the best course of action.

We take great pains to help the seller look into the mirror and examine his needs and those of his business. We help him formulate his objectives in an all-encompassing way. Only then do we suggest a course of action.

If the recommendation is to merge or sell (sometimes it is

not), our attention turns to identifying the "best" buyers. Many factors, ranging from business philosophies to price-earnings ratios, are weighed. We can help the seller expand his opportunities well beyond those random situations that at first blush appear so attractive.

One of our first steps is to draw upon our *buyer date bank.* This consists of punch cards containing firsthand information on the acquisition interests of more than 1,000 corporations who are seeking acquisitions. Their interests are classified by the Standard Industrial Classification (S.I.C.) code numbers of the types of companies they seek.

Pooling this output with our own knowledge of trends in acquisitions and trends in industry, and our knowledge of the seller's objectives, we produce a list of potential acquirers or merger partners for the selling company. We discuss in detail with each seller our reasons for recommending each potential purchaser.

If the seller then authorizes us to do so, we establish top-level contact with the potential buyer and arrange for preliminary meetings. Our assistance continues in a great variety of ways, but possibly in none more important than evaluating a purchaser's offer or working out appropriate counter-offers.

Watch Out for Later Problems

Going public, as seen, has some advantages and some drawbacks. Some of the disadvantages become apparent only *after* you have taken the big plunge.

One is failure of the underwriter, whether a full SEC offering or one under Reg A, to maintain an "aftermarket." When stocks trade over the counter, some firm must maintain a market by actually buying when people or people's brokers offer shares for sale, and the firm must sell—short if necessary—when people want to buy. The underwriter must, in other words, keep a store in the stock, with shares on the shelf.

It's a temptation when going public to make an intrastate offering, to residents of one state only. That way you avoid some red tape, but you will almost never get an aftermarket because the type of firm that goes in for intrastate offerings is seldom financially strong enough to keep up a market after flotation of the issue.

Another little trap you discover after going public inside a single state is that the company—not merely the distribution to stockholders—must do business largely within the single state. The Securities and Exchange Commission's rule says that to be exempt from its scrutiny, 80 percent of sales volume must be inside the state to whose residents the shares were offered.

Business Week's March 18, 1972, issue told the story of some after-going-public troubles. Bylined by William G. Shepherd, Wall Street editor, the article stated: "Going Public Can Hurt."

> When a new stock issue comes out at 5 and instantly soars to 15, there's a serious question whether the shares were initially priced too low, perhaps so that Wall Street and the speculators could grab most of the loot themselves. Small companies thinking about going public in this year's bubbling market might consider the experiences of their predecessors. Typical gripes:
> "Our underwriter raped us," reports the president of a small New York company that sold $250,000 in stock in 1968. "He took 10 percent in cash right off the top. Also, he received $10,000 for nonaccountable expenses. Finally, he received warrants to buy 30,000 shares for which he paid a penny apiece. This represents about 11 percent of our total capitalization." Further, the president says, "he's not even making a market in our stock." The head of a Boston company says underwriters "are not much better than horse traders and don't really care about the companies they underwrite."
> Manhattan public relations man Art Stevens surveyed about five hundred companies that went public in 1968-69. He found that, for 79 percent of the companies, the stock offering provided only two years' worth of capital—and frequently less. Some 44 percent felt that their underwriters didn't do all they

could do or were supposed to do. Another big complaint: Market makers often abandon a stock after the initial trading enthusiasm dies. For the companies in the survey, the median number of market makers dropped from 6.4 to 5.1, and 24 percent now have three market makers or less. Then too, the 1970 bear market undermined the confidence of 16 percent in the benefits of going public. If they had the choice, 11 percent said they wouldn't do it again.

10: The Venture Capitalists

"V ENTURE," the dictionary says, is "a speculative or risky undertaking; something at hazard in such an undertaking; a stake or wager; to hazard; to brave dangers."

There are men and companies in the business of undertaking speculative and risky financial undertakings in hope of sizable gain. They form an important source of funds for a new business or introduction of new products and services.

Venture capitalists are people who take risks, putting up money with no (or little) visible collateral. Just the people you want to know when you're looking for capital to start a new business or expand an existing one.

The SBICs

Earlier, we met the Small Business Administration, which is a government organization. It is in the field of lending money. *Small Business Investment Corporations* are private organizations under the supervision of the SBA—but not with their money disbursement operations organized by it—which furnish venture capital.

139

Sometimes the venture capital they furnish is given in return for convertible debentures. A *debenture*, by definition, is an unsecured bond. When a debenture is convertible, it means that at the option of the holder—in the cases we're discussing that means at the option of the SBIC—the debenture can be converted into common stock.

With such a setup, a Small Business Investment Corporation can have the added security of a loan (the debenture) with option to change its investment into part ownership later should the venture succeed.

Let experts from the Small Business Administration furnish details about SBICs. In a booklet appropriately called "SBIC," they pointed out:

> New SBICs derive their initial capital from private investors and normally become eligible to obtain funds from the government or from private financial institutions through government-guaranteed loans.
>
> An SBIC finances small firms in two general ways—by straight loans and by equity-type investments which give the SBIC actual or potential ownership of a portion of a small business's stock. All financings must be for at least five years, except that a borrower may elect to prepay indebtedness.
>
> SBICs invest in practically all types of manufacturing and service industries and in a wide variety of other types of businesses, including construction, retailing, and wholesaling. Many seek out small businesses offering new products or services because they believe these firms have unusual growth potential.
>
> Some SBICs specialize in electronics companies, research and development firms, or other types of businesses regarding which the SBICs management has special knowledge. Most companies diversify and will consider a wide variety of investments.
>
> SBICs are intended to be profit-making corporations. Their major function is to make "venture" or risk investments by supplying equity capital and extending unsecured loans and

loans not fully collateralized to worthy small enterprises. Some SBICs have been organized and utilized as subsidiaries, on a profit-making basis, by national concerns to provide equity capital and long-term funds to minority enterprises and co-ordinate volunteer business counseling, legal aid, and management training for the benefit of such enterprises and the benefit of the business community. . . .

Small businesses generally have difficulty obtaining equity capital to finance their growth. Without up-to-date operating records and strong financial statements, small business concerns have difficulty in obtaining long-term financing.

To help close this financing gap, Congress passed the Small Business Investment Act of 1958, which authorized SBA to license, regulate, and help finance privately organized and privately operated SBICs, which in turn would provide equity-type and long-term financing to small concerns. . . .

In general, SBA considers a firm to be "small" and therefore eligible for SBIC financing if its assets do not exceed \$5 million, if its net worth is not more than \$2.5 million, and if its average net income after taxes for the preceding two years was not more than \$250,000. If a business does not qualify as small under these provisions, it may qualify under certain other criteria established by SBA for its business loan program, or for assistance to firms that are located in areas of substantial unemployment. In determining the size of a business, SBA also considers the size of any affiliates, including a parent company that controls the firm, and any other companies controlled by the same parent company.

A list of SBICs is given in Appendix 2.

The Banker as Venture Capitalist

It surprises those with an old view of the banker as a portly, conservative lender on only the best security to learn that in the seventies, banks' trust departments are investing in ventures.

In a November 1970 article, "Bank Trusts, the New Venture Capitalists," *Finance Magazine* noted that:

Today . . . banks and other financial institutions are showing new interest in venture capital undertakings. U.S. Trust, for
one, is "seriously considering" placing some of its pension funds
into a professional venture capital company which would, in
turn, invest the money for the bank and other subscribers into
new enterprises. "It depends on who the people are behind the
[venture capital] company," explains Mr. Hollerieth. "Venture
capital is a highly specialized field, and we don't profess to be
experts in it," he continues, adding: "But some people are
qualified and in a strong position to recognize good situations.
This is the kind of advice we would seek."

Mr. Hollerieth isn't alone in this respect. A number of
financial executives with banks, trust companies, and insurance
firms are coming to the same conclusion. Sometimes at client
request and largely to get better performance from some of
their pension dollars, they are turning to professional management firms to put them in the venture capital field. The
amounts being managed by persons outside their organization
is small but promises to grow as investor interest in venture
capital undertakings continues to mushroom.

For example, First National City Bank and two Midwestern
banks, along with a few other institutional investors, put up the
$81 million to float Heizer Corp., a Chicago-based venture
capital company. So far, the company has invested only about
$10 million in a half-dozen or more companies, but it expects to
add another 10 or 20 to this portfolio in the next year. Another
new venture company, Newcourt Securities Co., raised $50
million recently with the backing of banking and institutional
money. Moreover, like Mr. Hollerieth, the heads of bank trust
departments are finding themselves inundated with literature,
phone calls, and personal visits from venture capital companies promising to multiply their trust dollars by backing
promising new ventures. Notes John C. Sutherland, vice-
president of Irving Trust Co., "There have been so many
people in and out of my office lately with investment proposals
that it is hard to keep track of them all."

The term *venture capital* means many things to many people,
and there are a great variety of firms in the business, from

investment bankers and private partnerships to, more recently, large corporations and insurance companies. Generally, it might be defined as providing high-risk funds to underwrite new, potentially high-growth enterprises. Sometimes this will involve providing so-called "seed money," which is pre-product or "idea" capital put in at the earliest stages in the formation of a new company. Or, other times it will involve production start-up money needed to get a firm rolling, or development- or expansion-stage funds that may be loaned to an existing company. In return, the investor gets an equity interest in the company.

Venture Companies

In a speech before the Washington Society of Security Analysts, Don A. Christensen, president, and Mark Rollinson, vice-president and secretary of Greater Washington Investors, explained how a venture capital corporation works in furnishing new money to small businesses. Said Mr. Christensen:

> At Greater Washington we are involved in the most exciting business that one could imagine—participating in the creation of what could be tomorrow's Polaroid or Xerox or Digital Equipment Corporation. We call this venture capital.
>
> I view venture capital as a melding together of the money and experience within Greater Washington with the talents and creative energies of an outside management group to create a substantial enterprise. Basically, it is a dynamic and creative activity, which brings together a number of factors to achieve an objective.
>
> Another way of describing our business is that which Mark Rollinson uses. He describes Greater Washington's role as that of a professional minority investor in technological growth enterprises.
>
> Each of the words in his definition has significance. Professional—as I will describe later, we have the experience and skills that indeed qualify us as professional. Second, we are a minority investor. There are a number of investors willing to

enter into technological enterprises on a control basis. In this regard Greater Washington is quite special. We stand ready to assist our companies actively whenever they desire it, but we do not manage them. Rather, we seek to invest only where a strong management—one of proven ability and integrity—already exists. Finally, the last part of his definition concerns our emphasis on technological growth companies. We invest in technology, and for a reason. We see within technology the elements of great opportunity for small companies. We believe that the technological developments of the past decade, and of the coming decades, offer the opportunity for small companies, for dedicated management groups, to build something of substantial value, and here we see our opportunity.

In 1959, when Greater Washington was being organized, institutional sources of venture capital largely did not exist. There were a few partnerships engaged in venturing, the Whitneys and the Rockefellers, for example. There was also one publicly owned venture capital company, American Research and Development; however, as an over-the-counter company with less than $15 million in capital, even it was relatively unknown. (How different it is today now that ARD's $15 million in capital has grown to more than $350 million!) . . .

Together, there have been a total of 62 companies in the GWII portfolio. A number of these were totally new ventures; others, although young, possessed at least a limited operating history; and some were relatively mature companies into which earlier GWII portfolio companies had merged. In nearly every case we have worked closely with our portfolio company managements in meeting the inevitable corporate problems that a growing company faces. We have been through public offerings, mergers, acquisitions, reorganizations, and liquidations; we have counseled them when they built new plants or introduced new product lines; and we have helped them recruit and develop their management talent. In short, we have been through the trials and tribulations, as well as the achievements, of building a business—not once, but many times. It is this experience—and the skills that we have developed from it—that constitutes Greater Washington's greatest strength.

Money per se is easy to come by for any valid enterprise and often can be obtained at a lower apparent cost from some other source. However, when a company takes GWII as its minority partner, in addition to GWII's financial backing it has access to all the experience and expertise that we have developed over the past ten years of venturing. . . .

Today Greater Washington's portfolio companies are located throughout the nation and are engaged in a wide spectrum of industries. We have portfolio companies engaged in building computers and their related equipment; in applying electronics to problems of education, communications, defense, and industrial control; and in developing new products and processes to meet the needs of our technological society. Typically, our companies are operating in areas where there is a high degree of technological change since it is here that major opportunities are found. They are embarked upon strategies to exploit these opportunities—strategies which, if successful, will build value through growth in sales, profits, markets, and managements. As venture capitalists, we stand to share in these increased values, and it is through their realization that Greater Washington expects to reward its shareholders.

Mark Rollinson described the attitudes with which such a venture company as Greater Washington greets a new capital opportunity (although Greater Washington is technology-oriented, other companies are not, and a similar scene can be imagined in the offices of venture capitalists operating in different areas):

Imagine yourself looking at a deal brought in by one of your associates—call him "Mike"—a small, private placement deal. From the facts presented to you on paper you make the following accurate comments:
"Mike, this so-called company, Maryland Telecommunications, is operating literally out of a three-car garage! Why, I understand you have to sit on packing crates in the reception area. And these superior television cameras they make—the

ones that will see in the dark and still give picture resolution better than any camera system in existence—well if there's such a demand for those, why aren't they selling more? Why aren't their competitors—RCA, Dage, Westinghouse, and others making the same stuff? There's no patent protection on these allegedly proprietary developments, so if it ever takes off, the big guys will copy it. And you know the little fellow doesn't have a chance when the really big money comes in.

"Management? The president has never run anything on a large scale. He doesn't even come from a good college. One of the key employees is a chronic alcoholic. There's no depth. They have no comptroller.

"In addition, they're selling to a few OEM's. You know how fast that business can be cut off. And they are heavily involved in one application—medical fluoroscopy. The big boys are going to dominate medical electronics.

"Mike, this is the worst deal you've ever brought in. I think you need a little rest. Why don't you take a few days off?"

As it turns out, MTI suffered in varying degrees from all the hazards this imaginary analyst observed. But the quality of management reflected in MTI's product design, internal systems, purchasing policies, personnel policies, and the like sold GWII on the future in MTI.

I made an unsolicited call on MTI in January 1964 and in fact sat on a packing crate in a three-car garage while waiting to see the president.

In March of that year GWII invested $100,000 in MTI common stock at 15x estimated earnings. Our $100,000 doubled the company's net worth, and we got only 10 percent of the equity! In addition, we committed to lend MTI $200,000, and we purchased from the Small Business Administration a $70,000 low interest note in order to free MTI from some of the highly restrictive elements of its agreement with SBA.

Within two years MTI experienced all of the problems cited above and, in addition, lost its largest single customer (30 percent of sales), moved to a new plant, won a very close union election, and had to raise $1 million additional capital.

Despite these problems, the company kept right on doubling its sales every year and making approximately 11 percent profit—after taxes! MTI's management was superb!

GWII had an active role in consulting (for free) with MTI management during these years. In some matters, such as negotiating the company's underwriting and later its merger with KMS Industries, GWII actually represented the company, at the company's request.

To date we have realized more than $400,000 profit on our net investment in MTI (after debt repayment) of $200,000, and we have more than $1 million unrealized gain yet to be taken.

Another result of our field efforts to find deals was our investment in Tresco, a Philadelphia-based manufacturer of precision electronic transformers and specialized transducers.

In December 1965, when GWII invested in Tresco, the company was ready to embark on a major expansion program, both of physical plant and additional products. With GWII's investment of $250,000 in convertible debentures, Tresco's sales went from $2 million to $6 million in two years! GWII also assisted Tresco in obtaining $800,000 of additional public funds and a larger line of bank credit.

Tresco's management systems were not up to the strain. Large investory imbalances developed; planning and production systems were not streamlined; communications among the company's three plants broke down. Consequently, the company grew in volume but not in profits.

An executive committee of the Tresco board was formed, and GWII was asked to participate. After several months of hard work the committee concluded that major injections of new management were needed and that merger was the surest way of obtaining such management.

A nearby integrated circuit manufacturer, Solid State Scientific, only a year old but already profitable, wanted to "back into" being publicly held. Tresco's potentially strong earnings base appeared to offer some stability to complement the more erratic integrated circuit business. . . .

An extremely interesting new venture for GWII is the

Creare Corporation. Creare is unique for us in the sense that when we invested there was no management at all! (We have since recruited an excellent team.) Our September 1968 investment in Creare is our first commitment in the real estate development field, though we amended our investment policy to permit such ventures in 1965. . . .

Creare's first effort, now supported by a $1 million investment by GWII and a $1.250 million loan from Maryland National Bank, is in Pascagoula, Mississippi, now undergoing a tremendous boom as a result of current expansion in the area of operation of Litton, Thiokol, Bausch & Lomb, Standard Oil, and various supporting industries.

How much money is around for venture investors to put out? A lot, according to Benno C. Schmidt, managing partner of New York-based J.H. Whitney and Co. *Forbes Magazine* reported this expert's views and methods in a December 1, 1970, article, "The Money is There":

> According to Benno Schmidt, there is no shortage of venture capital. There's a shortage of genuine entrepreneurs. "It is almost easier to raise venture capital these days than to raise money for anything else," he says. What is scarce is the supply of promising entrepreneurs with promising ideas for building companies.
>
> "The rub in this business is that there just aren't very many men around like Kenny Spencer (of Spencer Chemical, now part of Gulf Oil) and Larry Spitters (of Memorex). So venture firms must attempt to succeed by backing men who are something less than entrepreneurial geniuses."
>
> In short, if the money men turn you down, it's probably because you and your idea are lousy. But how do smart money men decide whether you are really a promising entrepreneur or not?
>
> "It's all the attributes that separate any outstanding man from the average man," says Schmidt. "Keen intellect, stamina, the ability to attract and move people, sort out ideas, and avoid wasting time on ancillary or auxiliary matters.

"A man's idea counts, too, of course," says Benno Schmidt. "But ideas are a dime a dozen. What impressed me about men like Spitters and Spencer was that I could see they had the staying power to see their ideas through."

In the end, Schmidt concedes, he venture capitalist must make up his mind largely through a process of intuitive reasoning, based on his experience in backing other companies. That means he is sometimes going to make mistakes, turning down good men and backing poor ones. Schmidt himself freely admits that the process isn't infallible even for old hands like himself.

"At least half of the things we've done have not been, in hindsight, what I would call good investments," concedes Schmidt. "That doesn't mean that we lost everything, but it does mean that we had to settle for a loss or, at best, very little gain.

"You are all right as long as your successes do much better than your failures do badly," Schmidt says, and he turns to baseball for an analogy. Babe Ruth, Mickey Mantle, and other home-run hitters had a tendency to strike out frequently, but their heavy slugging more than offset that. "In our business, too," says Schmidt, "the home runs are usually so much more productive that you don't worry too much about a lot of strikeouts."

Schmidt stops short of revealing the actual profits J.H. Whitney has earned on investments like Memorex and Spencer Chemical. But he emphasizes that the prospective gains must be huge to justify the risks. "Today you can put your money into reasonably sound securities with a 10 percent annual return," he points out. "Taking into consideration the added risk in venture capital, you ought not be in the business if you can't achieve at least an average 20 percent-a-year return." After balancing the home runs against the strikeouts, a venture firm, he suggests, should be able at least to double its money every four years.

Another expert is venture capitalist Bill Hack, vice-president of F.S. Smithers and Co. in New York (branches at Dallas, Chicago, and San Francisco). Says Hack:

Venture capital is a risky business. The major and continuing effort of any professional venture capitalist is to follow certain disciplines in an effort to increase the odds in favor of the investor—by reducing the risk and improving the return—by actions taken both before the investment decision is made and afterward.

In the course of many years of experience F.S. Smithers & Co., Inc., has developed comprehensive techniques for the care and assistance of new ventures. This is done with a continuing involvement of our total organization. Not all ventures have been as successful as the original financing of IBM back in 1911, but our overall record is quite impressive, and we would be pleased to discuss it with you.

Our method of approach is as follows:

We look for growth areas offering the possibility of establishing a viable and profitable company or through expanding existing companies, by the application of modest amounts of money. We concentrate principally in the area of new technological developments since we believe greater opportunities for major growth are generated in these areas.

Assuming general interest, the first major investigation is of the people involved. We look at their abilities, motivations, leadership qualities, the background and balance of the team, and particularly of the key man. References, prior employers, and other sources are checked. The deal is dropped if the team and its leaders do not check out well.

Next, we look closely at the proposed operation and particularly the key advantage offered by the group and on which it expects to capitalize. An ongoing, profitable, expanding business must be the eventual result. We are not interested in a temporary advantage that quickly withers from competition, or a non-basic technology that readily can be duplicated.

Here, as in personal investigation, all of the resources of Smithers are used, particularly our technically competent research people. As needed, outside consultants are employed.

Assuming the project passes these initial stages of investigation and evaluation, a commitment letter is then written. This letter reflects not only considered judgment of the fair proportion of the company that should go to the new investors but also other pertinent considerations, such as board membership, new personnel to balance the team, and a detailed outline of the direction of the company with clearly defined goals.

The proper investigation and structuring of an investment is important, but this is only the start of the job. No venture, first-, second-, or third-stage, is without problems. Smithers assumes a partnership role in any venture capital situation that it assists in financing. It offers the continuing assistance of an investment banking team, which includes personnel with substantial operating management experience.

These people, having actually dealt with the problems of starting and expanding a small company to profitable levels, can help anticipate and provide solutions to problems that arise in a small venture—thus increasing the possibility of success. Many groups attracted by the potential profits in ventures have overlooked the importance of this active partnership role played by the seasoned venture capitalist, and with unfortunate results.

In addition to management consulting services, Smithers provides traditional investment banking services as the company moves toward public ownership.

We believe that when the proper disciplines are followed, venture capital situations can be most attractive. Contrary to majority opinion that rules against venture capital investments in the present economic situation, we believe that now is an excellent time for making those investments in smaller companies that, in our opinion, should have great potential growth in the seventies.

An unusual kind of venture capital is promoted by Bagert and Co., a San Francisco investment banking firm. Its idea is to assist small companies that seek to become large firms through capital for expansion. The method? Incorporation, and sale of stock to company employees.

The Establishment Helps Out
Who would expect General Electric to provide risk capital for

small businesses? It does this. So do others of the American economic establishment. T. Walton Storm, whose office is in the GE Building in New York, receives as many as ten capital investment proposals daily. He tries to talk to all of those who approach GE through a subsidiary, Business Development Services. The hope is that enough will succeed to be later candidates for acquisition by General Electric.

Standard Oil of New Jersey has a venture subsidiary called Jersey Enterprises, Inc., headed by H.E. McBrayer. As of 1972, it had made investments of $200,000 to $500,000 in four new companies.

Herbert Brinberg is in charge of a similar investment venture of American Can Co. Since 1971, when it was started, this sideline of American Can has put money into fledgling firms in the consumer research, chemical, and information storage and retrieval fields.

Emerson Electric had a subsidiary set up in 1970. It invests close to Emerson's home area, in circuitry and semi-conductors, but one effort financed by Emerson is in modular homes. Emerson's angle? "If it succeeds, we'll have a market for wiring," one executive noted.

Unlike General Electric and Standard Oil (New Jersey), many companies hide their efforts lest they be besieged by crank schemes. It has been estimated that more than a score of industrial giants offer seed money to selected new companies. It will be worth an approach to the big boys in the field selected for *your* new venture.

11: Maximum Mileage from the Money You Have

You may already have enough capital to get that business started—and not even know it. That kind of capital is like a buried treasure. You have to dig to find it.

The purpose of this chapter is to map out where to dig and to suggest some tools to use.

Avoid Credit Losses and Tie-Ups

An obvious way to do this is by using the big bank credit systems, BankAmericard and Master Charge, rather than financing your own charge accounts and other customer credit. Financing your own accounts means tying up capital and running the risk of loss.

One merchant who ignored these dangers, citing the service charges he was able to assess customers on time purchases, was warned that he was not in the banking business and, unless as large as Sears, Montgomery Ward, or the bigger downtown department stores, he would do better to leave credit to lenders and utilize his capital where it would do

more good. "The warning was worthless," reported a
management consultant who had been called in to prescribe
for the business's chronic cash shortages. "His eyes glittered
with interest charges instead of merchandise profits. Within
six months he had not enough working capital to obtain new
purchases and therefore was without the merchandise on
which the seemingly important interest and service charge
could be assessed. The result was the eventual closing of the
business."

Writing on "The Nation-Spanning Credit Cards," experts
of the Federal Reserve Bank of Chicago noted in their Bank's
March 1972 *Monthly Review*:

> Despite the rapid expansion, credit cards still represent only
> a minor part of total bank credit and total consumer credit. In
> mid-1971, they accounted for a little over 1 percent of all bank
> credit and for 9 percent of bank consumer lending. At the
> same time, they accounted for 3 percent of total consumer
> credit (bank and non-bank).
>
> A more significant comparison can be made by measuring
> credit-card credit against the yardstick of total consumer
> revolving credit—a field dominated up to now by retail charge
> accounts and department-store revolving-credit plans. Bank
> cards now make up 23 percent of revolving-credit outstand-
> ings, accounting for one-half of the total increase in this field
> during the last three years. This shift is not surprising since
> credit cards have been expressly designed to supplement or
> replace credit formerly carried by retailers.
>
> The rapid acceptability of credit cards bears witness to their
> usefulness to consumers. They provide a convenient charge-
> account service, with revolving-credit privileges, at a large
> number of retail outlets. On the basis of national and (more
> recently) international interchange plans, they can serve as
> travel-and-entertainment cards—and without the annual mem-
> bership fee required for regular T&E cards. They can be used
> in most cases to borrow up to $500 in cash, with repayment on a
> revolving basis if desired. They can provide protection in some

cases against overdrawn checking accounts through the use of automatic cash advances when insufficient funds are in the account. . . .

What merchants get—banks are just as active in signing up merchants as they are in signing up cardholders. The two national interchange systems had over one million merchant members on their rolls in mid-1971. The total, although containing some duplications, indicates the broad coverage of bank plans.

Merchants find bank cards advantageous because of their relatively low cost in relation to retailers' plans. Nationally, banks charge an average 3.5 percent discount on credit-card sales, and they also shoulder bad debt and fraud losses. Some merchants, especially travel-oriented merchants, find the honoring of bank cards to be a useful way of attracting customers. Most airlines and oil companies accept bank cards as well as their own simply because of the number of cardholders who are potential customers.

As in the case of many other competitive devices, some merchants encounter higher net costs when they are forced by competitive pressures to enroll in bank-card plans, where the extra business generated fails to compensate for the cost of discounted sales drafts. More typically, however, merchants are happy enough to replace their own credit with bank credit offered at a 3.5 percent average discount, particularly since most bank-card transactions occur in lines where credit has been traditionally available. . . .

One of the most striking features of the credit-card scene is the consolidation of most bank-card plans into two nationwide systems—National BankAmericard, Inc. (NBI), and Interbank, Inc. Until 1966, almost all card plans operated independently of each other. But in that year, Bank of America announced plans for the national licensing of its BankAmericard, which hitherto had been limited to California. In response, several other large banks announced the formation of a second coast-to-coast card system, Interbank.

With national interchange, the cardholder can use his card for purchasing goods in areas served by other banks. The interchange arrangement provides a means of transferring sales drafts from the merchant's bank to the cardholder's bank for collection, and thus of transforming local cards into national cards. The interchange arrangement increases the usefulness of cards to customers, and the greater number of potential users makes cards more attractive to merchants. Also, it encourages the formation of new plans and increases competitive pressures on individual banks to hasten the introduction of new plans of their own. The development of national card systems thus has helped bring about the sharp upsurge in card usage.

The form of the two interchange systems has stabilized in the last two years, and has centered around the use of two national cards, BankAmericard and Master Charge. In the process, the two systems have grown to parallel each other, with BankAmericard adopting a cooperative form of organization similar to Interbank, and Interbank in effect adopting a standard card design.

NBI, the corporation owned by the various BankAmericard issuers, was established in 1970 to replace Bank of America in the licensing and co-ordinating role for BankAmericard. In the first years after 1966, Bank of America had the expertise lacked by the new licensees and thus dominated BankAmericard. But this situation was temporary. Licensees soon began to operate on their own, and several large banks with fully operational plans adopted BankAmericard as a response to competitors' Master Charge cards, so that Bank of America eventually relinquished its central role and NBI took over its organizational responsibilities. Consequently, NBI and Interbank are now organized along the same corporate lines, except that NBI remains a somewhat more closely co-ordinated system.

Meanwhile, the Master Charge name and design were adopted by most Interbank members to ensure the increased nationwide acceptability of that plan. Originally, many Interbank members issued their own cards, each with a distinctive design but with only a small lowercase i within a circle to identify the card as an Interbank card. However, this feature was not distinctive enough to ensure the ready acceptability of such cards everywhere. Relatively quickly, most Interbank members adopted the Master Charge name and design for their cards. BankAmericard, having a standard design from the beginning, avoided the recognition problem.

Here are some pro and con pointers to consider about what has been called "plastic credit":

Pro: The bank, not your company, extends credit. Credit investigations take time and cost money. Through the big cards, however, you extend the credit without this bother and expense; the issuing banks check credit (and take the loss if they do so sloppily).

Pro: You get paid fast. With an ordinary credit set-up, the credit seller has to wait a month, frequently longer, to get in the credit he extended. Meanwhile, his employees must be paid regularly, and his suppliers look for their invoices to be honored on time. The result many times is a need for bank borrowings just to maintain accounts receivable. "It is capital that costs but doesn't pay," wailed the auditor for one firm. "And if we extend more credit we can count upon a certain percentage of that, too, being slow-pay—hence more bank borrowings and more capital uselessly tied up."

This is not true with a bank credit card. The customer may take months to pay the bank; in many cases the banks encourage this since they charge interest as high as 18 percent a year. But the merchant who accepts a bank's card is in most cases paid quickly so that none of his capital goes into accounts receivable.

Pro: Your volume is swelled by those who prefer to pay on time or use revolving credit. In its study "Credit and Credit Cards," the Federal Reserve Bank of San Francisco noted:

> When the customer is billed by his bank, he has two options available to him; he may either repay the full balance within a grace period (typically twenty-five days) without any service charge, or he may repay on revolving credit with interest charged on the unpaid balance. There are no other charges for

the credit card—the cards are issued free—nor is there any requirement to open an account with the bank. Thus, if a customer always pays within the grace period, the card is the equivalent of a charge account.

In practice, many customers choose the revolving-credit option, and their interest payments provide the bulk of banks' credit-card revenues. Merchant discounts, which were the major source of revenue for the early credit-card plans, are now less important.

Pro: People look for firms that accept the cards. With an estimated 20 million cards out—not all of them active, but enough to make the average payable balance of $185 look big—bank card holders constitute a sizable market. Convenience of the two cards has been widely advertised. It is demonstrable that some (and perhaps many) decisions on where to buy are made for the reason that Company A may accept cards and Company B may not.

Robert Johnston's study made for the Federal Reserve noted:

> For the customer, the bank credit card fits easily into habits already established by department-store and oil-company cards. In the public's mind, this is just another plastic credit card, but one with a greater acceptance at a number of different businesses. . . . Moreover, the organization that processes retail sales slips can be readily adopted to handle other transactions. Most credit-card plans now allow cardholders to borrow amounts up to $500, depending on the bank. Not only does this privilege enhance the usefulness of the card, but it allows the bank to process small loans more efficiently than it can through normal procedures.

Against these advantages, there are few—but weighty—disadvantages to consider before plumping for a bank credit card plan:

Con: The fee you pay to the bank. "True, it is not at the moment high," said one executive who talked against using bank credit cards. "Probably it costs less than to maintain any kind of records comparable to these. The thing that frightens me is that I have seen the banks' percentage raised. If they should decide to go ahead with raises to a level we considered un-workable, we would be in the position of the man who held a tiger by the tail—if we held on, we'd be hurt; if we let go, we'd be hurt because people would consider we had with-drawn a service to which they had a right."

Con: You must maintain an account with the issuing bank. Proc-ceeds from bank credit charges are put into an account at the bank whose card you accept—not at the bank of your choice. Some firms have long, continuing, pleasant relationships with non-card banks. It is not easy to break these. Nor is it easy to keep accounts at a bank of the company's choice, at the bank that issues BankAmericard, and again at the third bank that issues Master Charge plastic credit.

Con: You lose one form of contact with customers. "And a most important form," said the dealer quoted earlier. "It imper-sonalizes us. In this field, personal relationships are more important both to the customer and to the store than such relationships are in other areas."

Con: Suppose the bank's computer snarls? It is true that com-puters make few mistakes. But the mistakes they do make tend to be beauts—and often nearly uncorrectable. Computer technicians who are adept in programming their charges to solve problems and produce instant accounting are occasion-ally inept at correcting mistakes.

"A girl with a pencil can erase a mistake and re-enter correct figures," one disgruntled bank customer said after trying in vain for three months to produce an account correc-tion from the computer. "It doesn't seem to bother the girl with the pencil. She goes home at the end of the day and thinks no more of the erasure and correction. Not so a com-puter. The monster broods. It has a nervous breakdown com-bined with pip, mange, and sore feet."

When this happens to a customer's account he is justifiably angry. But not at the computer. At you.

Sometimes it is unavoidable to issue credit on your own. If that's the case, it is well to keep in mind that the customer who does not pay, or pays slowly, reduces your operating capital drastically. In its June 1972 issue the newsletter *BIZ* reported:

> Is a once-favorite customer or client now taking a half year to pay? This can make you borrow at high interest for a forced loan at no interest. Credit experts pass along these ideas for lessening the problem:
>
> 1. Dunning letters help, but a personal phone call to the slow payer does more. It is harder to squirm out of a voice confrontation than to ignore a letter. In the end, the slow payer probably needs you as much as you want to retain his orders.
>
> 2. Avoid future troubles with advance credit checks. The financial information you have may be old; a payer's means and habits change. To keep credit information current, talk to your bank or go directly to the customer for the latest certified financial statements.
>
> 3. Improving business conditions may lessen the slow-pay problem. But a customer who has formed a habit of putting off invoices will continue to do so in order to conserve his funds. Stopping the practice now means elimination of future trouble.

Cut Insurance Costs

Lowest-cost insurance is not always a policy that charges the smallest premiums. A danger not covered, or a procedure ignored that would make a claim questionable, is more costly than premium dollars. These can wreck a capital-building program by diverting money needed for expansion.

Experts from the U.S. Small Business Administration have prepared a checklist on business insurance:

Fire Insurance

1. You can add other perils—such as windstorm, hail, smoke, explosion, vandalism, and malicious mischief—to your basic fire insurance at a relatively small additional cost.

2. If you need comprehensive coverage, your best buy may be one of the all-risk contracts that offer the broadest available protection for the money.

3. The insurance company may indemnify you—that is, compensate you for your losses—in any one of several ways: (1) It may pay actual cash value of the property at the time of loss. (2) It may repair or replace the property with material of like kind and quality. (3) It may take *all* the property at the agreed or appraised value and reimburse you for your loss.

4. You can insure property you don't own. You must have an insurable interest—a financial interest—in the property *when a loss occurs* but not necessarily at the time the insurance contract is made. For instance, a repair shop or drycleaning plant may carry insurance on customers' property in the shop, or a person holding a mortgage on a building may insure the building although he doesn't own it.

5. When you sell property, you cannot assign the insurance policy along with the property unless you have permission from the insurance company.

6. Even if you have several policies on your property, you can still collect only the amount of your actual cash loss. All the insurers share the payment proportionately. Suppose, for example, that you are carrying two policies—one for $20,000 and one for $30,000—on a $40,000 building, and fire causes damage to the building amounting to $12,000. The $20,000 policy will pay $4,800; that is, . . . two-fifths of $12,000. The $30,000 policy will pay $7,200, which is . . . three-fifths of $12,000.

7. Special protection other than the standard fire policy is needed to cover the loss by fire of accounts, bills, currency, deeds, evidences of debt, and money and securities.

8. If an insured building is vacant or unoccupied for more than sixty consecutive days, coverage is suspended unless you have a special endorsement to your policy canceling this provision.

9. If, either before or after a loss, you conceal or misrepresent to the insurer any material fact or circumstance concerning your insurance or the interest of the insured, the policy may be voided.

10. If you increase the hazard of fire, the insurance company may suspend your coverage even for losses not originating from the increased hazard. (An example of such a hazard might be renting part of your building to a drycleaning plant.)

11. After a loss, you must use all reasonable means to protect the property from further loss or run the risk of having your coverage canceled.

12. To recover your loss, you must furnish within sixty days (unless an extension is granted by the insurance company) a complete inventory of the damaged, destroyed, and undamaged property showing in detail quantities, costs, actual cash value, and amount of loss claimed.

13. If you and the insurer disagree on the amount of loss, the question may be resolved through special appraisal procedures provided for in the fire-insurance policy.

14. You may cancel your policy without notice at any time and get part of the premium returned. The insurance company also may cancel at any time with a five-day written notice to you.

15. By accepting a coinsurance clause in your policy, you get a substantial reduction in premium. A coinsurance clause states that you must carry insurance equal to 80 or 90 percent of the value of the insured property. If you carry less than this, you cannot collect the full amount of your loss, even if the loss is small. What percent of your loss you can collect will depend on what percent of the full value of the property you have insured it for.

16. If your loss is caused by someone else's negligence, the insurer has the right to sue this negligent third party for the amount it has paid you under the policy.

17. A building under construction can be insured for fire, lightning, extended coverage, vandalism, and malicious mischief.

Liability Insurance

1. Legal liability limits of $1 million are no longer considered high or unreasonable even for a small business.

2. Most liability policies require you to notify the insurer immediately after an incident on your property that might

cause a future claim. This holds true no matter how unimportant the incident may seem at the time it happens.

3. Most liability policies, in addition to *bodily* injuries, may now cover *personal* injuries (libel, slander, and so on) *if* these are specifically insured.

4. Under certain conditions, your business may be subject to damage claims even from trespassers.

5. You may legally be liable for damages even in cases where you used "reasonable care."

6. Even if the suit against you is false or fraudulent, the liability insurer pays court costs, legal fees, and interest on judgments *in addition* to the liability judgments themselves.

7. You can be liable for the acts of others under contracts you have signed with them. This liability is insurable.

Automobile Insurance

1. When an employee or a subcontractor uses his own car on your behalf, you can be legally liable even if you don't own a car or truck yourself.

2. Five or more automobiles or motorcycles under one ownership and operated as a fleet for business purposes can generally be insured under a low-cost fleet policy against both material damage to your vehicle and liability of others for property damage or personal injury.

3. You can often get deductibles of almost any amount—say $250 or $500—and thereby reduce your premiums.

4. Automobile medical-payments insurance pays for medical claims, including your own, arising from automobile accidents regardless of the question of negligence.

5. In most states you must carry liability insurance or be prepared to provide other proof (surety bond) of financial responsibility when you are involved in an accident.

6. You can purchase uninsured-motorist protection to cover your own bodily injury claims from someone who has no insurance.

7. Personal property stored in an automobile and not attached to it (for example, merchandise being delivered) is not covered under an automobile policy.

Workmen's Compensation

1. Common law requires that an employer (1) provide his employees a safe place to work, (2) hire competent fellow employees, (3) provide safe tools, and (4) warn his employees of an existing danger.

2. If an employer fails to provide the above, under both common law and workmen's compensation laws he is liable for damage suits brought by an employee.

3. State law determines the level or type of benefits payable under workmen's compensation policies.

4. Not all employees are covered by workmen's compensation laws. The exceptions are determined by state law and therefore vary from state to state.

5. In about half the states, you are not legally *required* to cover your workers under workmen's compensation. If you do not, however, you may lose some of your legal defenses in employee suits.

6. You can save money on workmen's compensation insurance by seeing that your employees are properly classified.

7. Rates for workmen's compensation insurance vary from 0.1 percent of the payroll for "safe" occupations to about 25 percent of the payroll for very hazardous occupations.

8. Most employers in most states can reduce their workmen's compensation premium cost by reducing their accident rates below the average. They do this by using safety and loss-prevention measures.

Desirable Coverages

Some types of insurance coverage, while not absolutely essential, will add greatly to the security of your business. These coverages include business-interruption insurance, crime insurance, glass insurance, and rent insurance.

Business-Interruption Insurance

1. You can purchase insurance to cover fixed expenses that would continue if a fire shut down your business—such as salaries to key employees, taxes, interest, depreciation, and utilities—as well as the profits you would lose.

2. Under properly written contingent business-interruption insurance, you can also collect if fire or other peril closes down

the business of a supplier or customer and this interrupts your business.

3. The business-interruption policy provides payments for amounts you spend to hasten the reopening of your business after a fire or other insured peril.

4. You can get coverage for the extra expenses you suffer if an insured peril, while not actually closing your business down, seriously disrupts it.

5. When the policy is properly endorsed, you can get business-interruption insurance to indemnify you if your operations are suspended because of failure or interruption of the supply of power, light, heat, gas, or water furnished by a public utility company.

Crime Insurance

1. Burglary insurance excludes such property as accounts, fur articles in a showcase window, and manuscripts.

2. Coverage is granted under burglary insurance only if there are visible marks of the burglar's forced entry.

3. Burglary insurance can be written to cover, in addition to money in a safe, inventoried merchandise and damage incurred in the course of a burglary.

4. Robbery insurance protects you from loss of property, money, and securities by force, trickery, or threat of violence on *or off* your premises.

5. A comprehensive crime policy written just for small businessmen is available. In addition to burglary and robbery, it covers other types of loss by theft, destruction, and disappearance of money and securities. It also covers thefts by your employees.

6. If you are in a high-risk area and cannot get insurance through normal channels without paying excessive rates, you may be able to get help through the FAIR plan or through the U.S. Department of Housing and Urban Development. Your state insurance commissioner can tell you where to get information about these plans.

Rent Insurance

1. You can buy rent insurance that will pay your rent if the property you lease becomes unusable because of fire or other

insured perils and your lease calls for continued payments in such a situation.

2. If you own property and lease it to others, you can insure against loss if the lease is canceled because of fire and you have to rent the property again at a reduced rental.

Group Health Insurance

1. Group health insurance costs much less and provides more generous benefits for the worker than individual contracts would.

2. If you pay the entire cost, individual employees cannot be dropped from a group plan unless the entire group policy is canceled.

3. Generous programs of employee benefits, such as group health insurance, tend to reduce labor turnover.

Disability Insurance

1. Workmen's compensation insurance pays an employee only for time lost because of work injuries and work-related sickness—not for time lost because of disabilities incurred off the job. But you can purchase, at a low premium, insurance to replace the lost income of workers who suffer short-term or long-term disability not related to their work.

2. You can get coverage that provides employees with an income for life in case of permanent disability resulting from work-related sickness or accident.

Retirement Income

1. If you are self-employed, you can get an income tax deduction for funds used for retirement for you and your employees through plans of insurance or annuities approved for use under the Self-Employed Individuals Tax Requirement Act of 1962 (Keogh Act).

2. Annuity contracts may provide for variable payments in the hope of giving the annuitants some protection against the effects of inflation. Whether fixed or variable, an annuity can provide retirement that is guaranteed for life.

Key-Man Insurance

1. One of the most serious setbacks that can come to a small

company is the loss of a key man. But your key man can be insured with life insurance and disability insurance owned by and payable to your company.

2. Proceeds of a key-man policy are not subject to income tax, but premiums are not a deductible business expense.

3. The cash value of key-man insurance, which accumulates as an asset of the business, can be borrowed against and the interest and dividends are not subject to income tax as long as the policy remains in force.

In addition to these items, there are the direct costs of insurance. Few buyers know that the cost of comparable life insurance policies can vary as much as 170 percent. That was brought out in a study by Dr. Herbert S. Denenberg, insurance commissioner of the state of Pennsylvania. Although figures will vary from state to state, Pennsylvania statistics are indicative of costs and returns in most areas.

Comparisons were made on straight life cash-value insurance. This, the report indicated, "combines insurance and protection. . . . The cash value increases each year. The rest is pure protection. . . . A $10,000 policy after twenty years may have $3,500 cash value; this is savings. The other $6,500 would be considered the insurance portion of the contract."

Denenberg stressed that "you can't tell which company is giving you the lowest cost by looking at premium alone. . . . Company A might have lower premiums than Company B, but Company B might pay larger dividends and have higher cash values."

The tests considered purchase at three ages. The first was male twenty or female twenty-three. The second was male thirty-five or female thirty-eight. The third was male age fifty or female age fifty-three.

In the first group, Connecticut Mutual Life Insurance Co. showed lowest cost, with Central Life Assurance Co. second and Home Life Insurance third.

In the middle group, Bankers Life Co. came out in top place (it was fourth in the first group), with Home Life

Insurance second and Northwestern Mutual Life Insurance Co. third.

In the final group, Bankers Life was number one, National Life Insurance Co. two, and Home Life Insurance Co. third.

Lessons learned, according to Dr. Denenberg:

— Shop for insurance as you would for potatoes or a new car.

— Premiums alone won't tell which policy costs less.

— If you already have a policy, it is usually a mistake to drop this for coverage in a new company.

Pay Key People in Non-Cash

In its September 1972 issue the newsletter *BIZ* reported:

Money is only the beginning, and frequently the least part, of executive compensation. Salary is subject to the grab of the Internal Revenue Department and its state equivalents. Gimmicks now being used to pad out the life of the upper-echelon executive are different.

Stock options are an obvious example. They compensate a man of ability by allowing him to purchase shares under the going market price, turning at least some of the future compensation into capital gains instead of ordinary income if he succeeds in lifting company profits and consequently the price of its stock. That is considered quite legit as long as the differential between market price of the stock and the price paid by executives buying on option is not too great. However, one West Coast company allows execs to buy at 10c per share stock trading on an Exchange at $50.

New ideas are developed every day for attracting top talent and keeping it happy. Many companies lend money at tiny interest rates to the top brass. Typical is a deal in which the company lent one VP $200,000 to buy an apartment structure, charging 2.5 percent.

Other members of the upper corporate class receive free houses—rationalization being that they carry on some business activities at home. Country club memberships, limousines, paid-up insurance policies are routine extra compensation.

Little-Known Cost-Cutting Ways

— On the U.S.-Mexican border at Nogales, 200 miles from my home in Scottsdale, Arizona, is a Samsonite plant that manufactures luggage brought across the border into the U.S. It utilizes lower-cost Mexican labor. The famous Barbie doll is made over the border in Mexicali. Kayser-Roth Corp. has three Mexican plants. Under its National Frontier Program, the government of Mexico will assist in setting up over-the-border businesses. Its assistance is not confined to corporate giants. At the time a 1972 survey was made, sample daily wages were $2.82 in Piedras Negras up to $4.32 in Tijuana.

— Some of your equipment can be met from government surplus. A typical offering circular might ask bids on an IBM typewriter, flagons of perfume, or three bulldozers. These bargains exist because professional purchasing executives sometimes over-buy. The United States government puts its buying mistakes up for repurchase.

General Services Administration and the Department of Defense will on request send notices of periodic surplus sales. Department of Defense offices are in Washington. GSA selling offices are in regions across the country. To find the one in which you're located, write General Services Administration, Washington. Lists include hard goods, furniture, office equipment, and tools.

"You must submit bids," noted the newsletter *BIZ* in its May 1972 issue, "and that's where a close judgment of the market for any given item can help. Overbid and you'll get what you're after, but not necessarily at a price that affords a bargain. Underbid and someone else will grab it from under your nose.

"Buyers must accept goods as is and where situated. That means no complaint if an item turns out to be junk and freight charges are high. GSA and DOD try to be honest. They describe items pretty much as they are. If you can visit the sale sites, you're better able to judge condition than by merely reading descriptions.

"Freight charges have to be added to the cost of each item. If something is shipped from Los Angeles to Lafayette, or Spokane to Shreveport, delivery is both slow and costly."

Best Temporary Returns on Surplus Cash

The term "surplus cash" seems out of place in a book on how to raise capital. It is not. In every business, cash accumulates temporarily while it awaits completion of a project unexpectedly late, a tax bill, or an expected expense.

If you let the money stay unproductively in a checking account, you miss out on an opportunity to make sometimes small but always helpful additions to—not temporary but *permanent*—capital.

The money can be put into Treasury bills with maturities of three, six, and twelve months. These are short-term obligations of the U.S. government and usually (but not always) pay more than bank savings rates or those available from savings and loan associations. You can buy them through a bank or broker where you are a regular customer.

There's a catch. Treasury bills come in minimum amounts of $10,000. For amounts smaller than that, or at times when bills bring in less than the 5 percent commonly available, try bank certificates of deposit. These are written in amounts of $1,000 and over and can be tailored to the bank customer's need. Most banks will write them for periods as short as thirty days.

A Financial Audit

In a *Management Aid* issued by the U.S. Small Business Administration, "Financial Audits: a Tool For Better Management," B. LaSalle Woelful of St. Edwards University, Austin, Texas, wrote (all businessmen's names disguised):

An independent audit of Tom Mapper's small company showed that he had not provided the control procedures necessary to safeguard his company's assets. The reason was that, being in business only a few years, he had concentrated all his efforts on production and sales.

Lacking internal control procedures, Mr. Mapper's company was exposed to unnecessary risks. For example, the audit revealed that the company's bank statement had not been reconciled with the company's books for the five months prior to the audit.

Fortunately, Mr. Mapper's employees were honest. Nevertheless, he had run the risk of overdrawing his account. It so happened that he thought he had $540 more than he actually had. This bookkeeping error was revealed only when a reconciliation was made.

To correct this and other weaknesses, the accountant who made the audit urged Mr. Mapper to adopt the following techniques of internal control:

(1) Organize his recordkeeping so that only qualified personnel would be responsible for recording financial and statistical data.

(2) Assign duties so that no one person would be in complete control of an entire transaction that involved handling cash or other assets.

(3) Make sure that his recordkeeping system gave him or another key executive control—a yes or no—over transactions.

In adopting these recommendations, Mr. Mapper did not have to hire any new employees. Several had to be retrained, however, in order to do the job in an efficient and economical manner.

When the accounts of Streeting and Company were audited, Mr. Streeting learned that his accounting procedures did not provide adequately for the control of cash.

This laxity was practically an invitation to his employees to be careless and even dishonest. To plug this possible leak, the accountant offered several recommendations.

First, Mr. Streeting should adopt methods that would get his cash under control immediately. To protect cash receipts, he was advised: (1) to separate the handling of cash from the recording of cash receipts (for example, the cashier should not be the same person as the bookkeeper); and (2) to deposit *all* cash receipts daily.

To control cash disbursements, the auditor advised Mr. Streeting: (1) to adopt the voucher system for all cash payments; (2) to make cash disbursements by prenumbered checks written on safety paper on a checkwriting machine; (3) to make one person responsible for preparing vouchers and checks and another for okaying them; and (4) to set up a petty cash fund so that small cash disbursements could be made only after proper authorization.

The auditor also insisted that Mr. Streeting, or someone other than the person responsible for the recordkeeping, prepare the monthly reconciliation of the company's bank statement. Thus a double check on cash receipts would be provided.

Finally, Mr. Streeting agreed to arrange for periodic surprise audits. This procedure was suggested after the independent auditor discovered that Mr. Streeting's bookkeeper had pocketed a cash payment of $85 that a customer had paid on his account.

The bookkeeper concealed his theft by not crediting the customer's account; in the next accounting period, he credited the account with a payment from a second customer—a practice called lapping. Surprise audits would discourage such practices.

Another owner-manager, Bill Polman, found additional working capital as a result of an audit. It showed that he had approximately $28,000 tied up in excessive inventory.

This fact was brought to light when the outside accountant supervised the inventory count. The count confirmed the existence of a declining rate of inventory turnover.

An analysis of purchasing and inventory control procedures led Mr. Polman to set up a centralized purchasing department. To run it, he hired an experienced purchasing agent who standardized certain parts that went into the product. Thus the assistant reduced the company's investment in materials. Mr. Polman also found that he could discontinue the manufacture of several slow-moving product lines that had lost their profit-making potential according to the auditor's cost studies.

Finally, with the help of the accountant, Mr. Polman installed a standard cost system. As a result, he was able to keep track of six important manufacturing costs by reading reports and asking the following questions:

Are *raw materials* being *purchased* at prices above or below standard prices? Are *raw materials* being used in *production* in amounts more than or less than allowed by standard?

Is *labor* being *paid* for at rates above or below standard? Is *labor* being used in *production* in amounts more than or less than allowed by standard?

Were actual manufacturing *overhead expenses* more than or less than the budget allowed at standard hours for work performed? Was there idle *plant capacity*; or was the plant used in excess of standard capacity?

The last story also deals with growth, but in a small company whose owner-manager, John Site, has learned that orderly expansion can be a way of life. He tried to reach the following growth objectives in his five-year-old company: (1) increased earning power, (2) increased assets, and (3) improvement in trade position.

In making long-range plans for these goals, Mr. Site has learned certain ground rules, such as deciding on how to finance expansion. He can get funds from internal sources, such as profits retained in his business, or from external sources, such as a loan. Over the years, audits have helped him decide that the best method for him is plowing profits back into the business.

Another ground rule that Mr. Site learned is deciding

which part of an expansion program should come first. He planned to add new product lines, to replace machinery and equipment, and to build a new plant.

To determine which he should do first, Mr. Site uses the following tests: (1) Which proposal promises the best rate of return on capital invested (anticipated profit divided by capital employed)? (2) Which proposal will most quickly recover through total cash flow (profits plus depreciation) the capital outlay?

In this manner, he is able to plan, administer, and control his expansion program. Thus in an orderly way he turns plans into assets on his company's balance sheet.

Appendix 1: Cities with Small Business Administration Offices

Agana, Guam
Albany, New York
Albuquerque, New Mexico
Anchorage, Alaska
Atlanta, Georgia
Augusta, Maine
Baltimore, Maryland
Birmingham, Alabama
Boise, Idaho
Boston, Massachusetts
Buffalo, New York
Casper, Wyoming
Charleston, West Virginia
Charlotte, North Carolina
Chicago, Illinois
Cincinnati, Ohio
Clarksburg, West Virginia
Cleveland, Ohio
Columbia, South Carolina
Columbus, Ohio

Concord, New Hampshire
Corpus Christi, Texas
Dallas, Texas
Denver, Colorado
Des Moines, Iowa
Detroit, Michigan
Eau Claire, Wisconsin
El Paso, Texas
Fairbanks, Alaska
Fargo, North Dakota
Fresno, California
Gulfport, Mississippi
Harlingen, Texas
Hartford, Connecticut
Hato Rey, Puerto Rico
Helena, Montana
Holyoke, Massachusetts
Honolulu, Hawaii
Houston, Texas
Indianapolis, Indiana

175

Jackson, Mississippi
Jacksonville, Florida
Kansas City, Missouri
Knoxville, Tennessee
Las Cruces, New Mexico
Las Vegas, Nevada
Little Rock, Arkansas
Los Angeles, California
Louisville, Kentucky
Lubbock, Texas
Madison, Wisconsin
Marquette, Michigan
Marshall, Texas
Memphis, Tennessee
Miami, Florida
Milwaukee, Wisconsin
Minneapolis, Minnesota
Montpelier, Vermont
Nashville, Tennessee
Newark, New Jersey
New Orleans, Louisiana
New York, New York

Oklahoma City, Oklahoma
Omaha, Nebraska
Philadelphia, Pennsylvania
Portland, Oregon
Providence, Rhode Island
Richmond, Virginia
Rochester, New York
St. Louis, Missouri
Salt Lake City, Utah
San Antonio, Texas
San Diego, California
San Francisco, California
Seattle, Washington
Sioux Falls, South Dakota
Spokane, Washington
Springfield, Illinois
Syracuse, New York
Tampa, Florida
Washington, District of
    Columbia
Wichita, Kansas
Wilmington, Delaware

Appendix 2: Addresses of Small Business Investment Corporations

Alabama

Investment Capital Corporation
57 Adams Avenue
Montgomery, Alabama 36103

Alaska

Alaska Business Investment
  Corporation
5th Avenue E Street, Box 600
Anchorage, Alaska 99501

Alaska Pacific Capital
  Corporation
Suite 710, 425 G Street
Anchorage, Alaska 99501

Alyeska Investment Company
  (M)*
1815 South Bragaw Street
Anchorage, Alaska 99506

Arizona

C.S.C. Capital Corporation
3003 N. Central Avenue,
  Suite 2406
Phoenix, Arizona 85102

First Southwest SBIC
1611 East Camelback Road
Phoenix, Arizona 85016

California

ABCD Equity Funds, Inc.
9220 Sunset Blvd., Suite 222
Los Angeles, California 90069

Arcata Investment Company
  (M)*
2750 Sand Hill Road
Menlo Park, California 94025

* M indicates a Minority Enterprise SBIC.

177

Arcata Investment Company
12911 Cerise Avenue
Hawthorne, California 90250

Bankers SBIC
301 20th Street
Oakland, California 94612

Bryan Capital, Inc.
235 Montgomery St.
San Francisco, California
94104

C S & W Investment Company
385 Grand Avenue
Oakland, California 94610

California Growth Capital, Inc.
1615 Cordova Street
Los Angeles, California 90007

Capital City Equity Company
2509 S. Broadway
Santa Ana, California 92701

City Capital Corporation
9255 Sunset Blvd.
Los Angeles, California 90069

City of Commerce Investment
Company (M)*
1117 B South Goodrich Blvd.
Los Angeles, California 90022

C.S.C. Capital Corporation
61 South Lake Street
Pasadena, California 91101

Continental Capital
Corporation
555 California St., 26th Fl.
San Francisco, California
94104

Creative Capital Corporation
Russ Building
San Francisco, California
94104

Crocker Capital Corporation
405 Florence Street
Palo Alto, California 94301

Developers Equity Capital
Corporation
9348 Santa Monica Blvd.
Beverly Hills, California
90210

Diversified Equities
Corporation
2401 Merced St.
San Leandro, California 94577

Edvestco, Inc.
150 Isabella Avenue
Atherton, California 94025

Equilease Capital Corporation
55 New Montgomery St.,
Suite 1
San Francisco, California
94105

Equilease Capital Corporation
315 South Beverly Drive
Beverly Hills, California 90212

First SBIC of California
621 S. Spring St., Suite 505
Los Angeles, California 90014

Goodwin SBIC
1200 First National Building
5th and B Street
San Diego, California 92101

---

* M indicates a Minority Enterprise SBIC.

H & R Investment Capital
Company
801 American Street
San Carlos, California 94070

Krasne Fund for Small
Business
9350 Wilshire Boulevard,
Suite 416
Beverly Hills, California 90212

North American Capital
Corporation
55 River Street, Suite 105
Santa Cruz, California 95060

Orange Coast Capital, Inc.
4533 MacArthur Blvd.
Newport Beach, California
92664

P.M. Investment Company
1000 Welch Road
Palo Alto, California 94304

Palo Alto Capital Company
(M)*
611 Hansen Way Bldg. 16
Palo Alto, California 94303

Pioneer Enterprises, Inc. (M)*
11255 W. Olympic Blvd.
Los Angeles, California 90064

Professional SBIC
5979 W. Third St.
Los Angeles, California 90036

Provident Enterprises
Corporation (M)*
81 Encina
Palo Alto, California 94301

Roe Financial Corporation
9885 Charleville Blvd.
Beverly Hills, California 90212

San Joaquin SBI Corporation
P.O. Box 5266
Santa Monica, California
90405

Small Business Enterprises
Company
555 California St.
San Francisco, California
94104

Space Age SBIC
1368 Lincoln Ave., Suite 111
San Rafael, California 94901

Sutter Hill Capital Corporation
2600 El Camino Real,
Room 500
Palo Alto, California 94306

Technology Capital
601 California St.
San Francisco, California
94108

Union America Capital
Corporation
445 S. Figueroa St.
Los Angeles, California 90017

Warde Capital Corporation
8907 Wilshire Blvd.,
Room 1012
Beverly Hills, California 90211

Warde Capital Corporation
3440 Wilshire Blvd.
Los Angeles, California

* M indicates a Minority Enterprise SBIC.

Wells Fargo Investment
  Company
475 Sansome St.
San Francisco, California
  94111

West Coast Capital Company
1240 High St., Suite B
Auburn, California 95603

Westamco Investment
  Company
7805 Sunset Blvd., Suite 201
Los Angeles, California 90046

Western Business Funds
235 Montgomery St.,
  Room 2200
San Francisco, California
  94104

Westland Capital Corporation
11661 San Vincente Blvd.
Los Angeles, California 90049

Colorado

Central Investment
  Corporation
Central Bank Building
Denver, Colorado 80202

Colorado SBIC, Inc.
P.O. Box 5168 T A
Denver, Colorado 80217

Equilease Capital Corporation
1701 W. 72nd Ave., Office
  No. 255
Denver, Colorado 80221

Connecticut

All State Venture Capital
  Corporation
855 Main St.
Bridgeport, Connecticut 06603

Business Ventures, Inc. (M)*
152 Temple St.
New Haven, Connecticut
  06510

Capital for Technology
  Corporation
325 State St.
New London, Connecticut 06320

Capital for Technology
  Corporation
70 Farmington Ave.
Hartford, Connecticut 06101

Connecticut Venture Capital
  Corporation
37 Lewis St.
Hartford, Connecticut 06114

Connecticut Capital
  Corporation
419 Whalley Ave.
New Haven, Connecticut
  06511

Conresco Corporation
10 River St.
Stamford, Connecticut 07901

Dewey Investment Corporation
18 Asylum St.
Hartford, Connecticut 06103

Equi Tronics Capital
  Corporation
1492 Highridge Road
Stamford, Connecticut 06903

_____

* M indicates a Minority Enterprise SBIC.

First Connecticut SBIC
177 State St.
Bridgeport, Connecticut 06603

First Miami SBIC
293 Post Road
Orange, Connecticut 06477

Hartford Community Capital
  Corporation (M)*
70 Farmington Ave.
Hartford, Connecticut 06101

Investors Capital Corporation
955 Main St.
Bridgeport, Connecticut 06603

Manufacturers SBIC of
  Connecticut
1488 Chapel St.
New Haven, Connecticut
  06511

Marwit Capital Corporation
19 West Elm St.
Greenwich, Connecticut 06830

Nationwide Funding
  Corporation
10 A Ambassador Dr.
Manchester, Connecticut
  06040

Northern Business Capital
  Corporation
79 Isaac St.
Norwalk, Connecticut 06850

Nutmeg Capital Corporation
125 Market St.
New Haven, Connecticut
  06510

SBIC of Connecticut
1115 Main St.
Bridgeport, Connecticut 06603

Transamerica Capital
  Corporation
19 W. Elm St.
Greenwich, Connecticut 06830

Delaware
Delaware Investment
  Company
200 W. 9th St., P.O. Box 188
Wilmington, Delaware 19801

D.C.
Allied Capital Corporation
1625 Eye Street, N.W.
Washington, D.C. 20006

Broad Arrow Investment
  Corporation
1701 Pennsylvania Ave., N.W.,
  Suite 1200
Washington, D.C. 20006

Capital Investment Company
  of Washington
1001 Connecticut Ave., N.W.
Washington, D.C. 20036

Distribution Services
  Investment Corporation
1725 K St., N.W.
Washington, D.C. 20006

Greater Washington Industrial
  Investments
1015 18th St., N.W., Suite 300
Washington, D.C. 20036

---

* M indicates a Minority Enterprise SBIC.

Minority Investments, Inc.
  (M)*
1200 U St., S.E.
Washington, D.C. 20020

Minority Investments, Inc.
  (M)*
1401 K St., N.W.
Washington, D.C. 20005

SBIC of New York, Inc.
1701 Pennsylvania Ave., N.W.
Washington, D.C. 20006

Florida

Atlantic Investment Fund, Inc.
150 S.E. Third Ave.
Miami, Florida 33131

Equilease Capital Corporation
3200 Ponce de Leon Blvd.,
  Room 218
Coral Gables, Florida 33134

First Miami SBIC
420 Lincoln Rd., Room 235
Miami Beach, Florida 33139

First North Florida SBIC
107 N. Madison St.
Quincy, Florida 32351

Gold Coast Capital
  Corporation
1451 N. Bayshore Dr.
Miami, Florida 33132

Growth Business Funds, Inc.
2100 E. Hallandale Beach
  Blvd.
Hallandale, Florida 33009

Gulf States Capital Corp.
3605 N. Davis
Pensacola, Florida 32503

Market Capital Corporation
P.O. Box 22667
Tampa, Florida 33622

SB Assist Corporation of
  Panama City
Beach State Bank Bldg.
Panama City, Florida 32401

Southeast SBIC, Inc.
100 S. Biscayne Blvd.
Miami, Florida 33131

Georgia

Citizens & Southern Capital
  Corporation
P.O. Box 4899
Atlanta, Georgia 30303

CSRA Capital Corporation
914 Ga. R.R. Bank Building
Augusta, Georgia 30902

Dixie Capital Corporation
2210 Gaslight Tower
Atlanta, Georgia 30303

Equilease Capital Corporation
1720 Peachtree St., N.W.
Atlanta, Georgia 30309

Fidelity Capital Corporation
290 Interstate No., Suite 120
Atlanta, Georgia 30339

First American Investment
  Corporation
300 Interstate No., Suite 450
Atlanta, Georgia 30339

* M indicates a Minority Enterprise SBIC.

Investors Equity, Inc.
11 Pryor St., Suite 922
Atlanta, Georgia 30303

Mome Capital Corporation
912 Main St.
Thomson, Georgia 30824

SBI Corporation of Georgia
11 Pryor St., N.W., Suite 516
Atlanta, Georgia 30303

Southeastern Capital SBIC
3204 First National Bank Bldg.
Atlanta, Georgia 30303

Hawaii

SBIC of Hawaii, Inc.
1575 South Beretania St.
Honolulu, Hawaii 96814

Idaho

Industrial Investment Corp.
413 W. Idaho St.
Boise, Idaho 83702

Industrial Investment Corp.
1020 Main St.
Buhl, Idaho 83316

Illinois

Abbott Capital Corporation
120 S. LaSalle St., Suite 1148
Chicago, Illinois 60603

Adams Street Capital, Inc.
209 S. LaSalle St., Suite 555
Chicago, Illinois 60604

Advance Growth Capital Corp.
401 Madison St.
Maywood, Illinois 60153

Amoco Venture Capital Co.
  (M)*
910 S. Michigan Ave.
Chicago, Illinois 60605

Business Capital Corp.
120 S. LaSalle St., Suite 656
Chicago, Illinois 60603

Central Capital Corporation
4 Madison St.
Oak Park, Illinois 60302

Chicago Equity Corp.
188 W. Randolph St.
Chicago, Illinois 60601

Combined Opportunities, Inc.
  (M)*
5050 N. Broadway
Chicago, Illinois 60640

Conill Venture Corp.
231 S. LaSalle St.
Chicago, Illinois 60604

Equilease Capital Corp.
2400 E. Devon
Des Plaines, Illinois 60018

First Capital Corporation of
  Chicago
One First National Plaza
Chicago, Illinois 60670

Illinois Capital Investment
  Corp.
135 S. LaSalle St.
Chicago, Illinois 60603

LaSalle Street Capital Corp.
150 S. Wacker Dr.
Chicago, Illinois 60606

North Central Capital Corp.

* M indicates a Minority Enterprise SBIC.

201 N. Main St.
Rockford, Illinois 61101

Republic Capital Corp.
33 N. LaSalle St.
Chicago, Illinois 60602

SB Management Investors,
Inc.
612 N. Michigan Avenue
Chicago, Illinois 60611

The Urban Fund, Inc. (M)*
1525 East 53rd St.
Chicago, Illinois 60035

Indiana

Central States Small Business
Corp.
Mezz. Fl. Industrial Bank
Bldg.
Fort Wayne, Indiana 46802

Great Lakes SBI Corporation
Box 285
Tipton, Indiana 46072

Indiana Capital SBIC, Inc.
927 S. Harrison St.
Fort Wayne, Indiana 46802

Indiana Capital SBIC, Inc.
Chamber of Commerce Bldg.
Indianapolis, Indiana 46204

Merchants Capital Corp.
1515 N. Senate Ave.
Indianapolis, Indiana 46202

Iowa

First American Capital Corp.
American Building
Cedar Rapids, Iowa 52401

Iowa Growth Investment Co.
American Building
Cedar Rapids, Iowa 52401

Kentucky

Equal Opportunity Finance,
Inc. (M)*
1202 S. 3rd St.
Louisville, Kentucky 40201

Louisiana

Commercial Capital, Inc.
P.O. Box 939
Covington, Louisiana 70433

Delta Capital, Inc.
550 Pontchartrain Dr.
Slidell, Louisiana 70458

Delta Capital, Inc.
837 Gravier St., Room 1410
New Orleans, Louisiana 70112

First SBIC of Louisiana, Inc.
756 Poydras St.
New Orleans, Louisiana 70130

First SBIC of Lafourche, Inc.
1614 South Bayou Dr.
Golden Meadow, Louisiana
70357

Mid-South Capital Corp.
312 Polk St.
Mansfield, Louisiana 71052

Royal Street Investment Corp.
520 Royal St.
New Orleans, Louisiana 70130

Southern SBIC, Inc.
8137 Oleander St.
New Orleans, Louisiana 70118

* M indicates a Minority Enterprise SBIC.

Maine

Massachusetts Capital Corp.
57 Exchange St.
Portland, Maine 04111

Maryland

Allied Capital Corporation
4801 Montgomery Lane
Bethesda, Maryland 20014

Aviation Growth Investments
7979 Old Georgetown Rd.
Bethesda, Maryland 20014

Baltimore Community
   Investment Co. (M)*
1102 Mondawmin Concourse
Baltimore, Maryland 21215

Capital Area Investors, Inc.
101 Light St.
Baltimore, Maryland 21202

Equilease Capital Corp.
6600 York Rd.
Baltimore, Maryland 21204

Interstate Business Investment
   Co.
233 Equitable Bldg.
Baltimore, Maryland 21202

Massachusetts

Arrow Investment Corporation
1051 Beacon St.
Brookline, Massachusetts
   02146

Atlas Capital Corp.
55 Court St., Suite 200
Boston, Massachusetts 02108

Beacon Capital Corp.
587 Beacon St.
Boston, Massachusetts 02215

Business Achievement Corp.
1 Court St.
Boston, Massachusetts 02108

Eastern Seaboard Investment
   Corp.
73 State St., Suite 208
Springfield, Massachusetts
   01103

Equilease Capital Corporation
393 Totten Pond Rd.,
   Suite 651
Waltham, Massachusetts 02154

Federal St. Capital Corp.
75 Federal St.
Boston, Massachusetts 02110

Financial Investors of Boston
185 Devonshire St.
Boston, Massachusetts 02108

First Capital Corp. of
   Boston
One Federal St.
Boston, Massachusetts 02110

Massachusetts Capital Corp.
One Boston Pl.
Boston, Massachusetts 02108

Massapoag Investment Corp.
1330 Beacon St.
Brookline, Massachusetts
   02146

Mutual SBI Corp.
31 St. James Ave., Room 357
Boston, Massachusetts 02116

* M indicates a Minority Enterprise SBIC.

New England Enterprise
  Capital Corp.
28 State St.
Boston, Massachusetts 02109

North American MESBIC, Inc.
  (M)*
114 State Street
Boston, Massachusetts 02109

Pilgrim Capital Corp.
10 Pleasant St.
Brookline, Massachusetts
  02146

Schooner Capital Corp.
155 Berkley St.
Boston, Massachusetts 02116

Worcester Capital Corp.
446 Main St.
Worcester, Massachusetts
  01608

Yankee Capital Corp.
77 Franklin Street
Boston, Massachusetts 02110

Michigan

Equilease Capital Corporation
6421 John R., Suite 513
Detroit, Michigan 48202

Michigan Capital & Service,
  Inc.
410 Wolverine Bldg.
Ann Arbor, Michigan 48108

Midwest SBIC
1921 First National Bldg.
Detroit, Michigan

Motor Enterprises, Inc. (M)*
3044 W. Grand Blvd.
Detroit, Michigan 48202

Pooled Resources Investment
  Minority Enterprises, Inc.
  (M)*
2900 W. Grand Blvd.
Detroit, Michigan 48202

SBIC of New York
770 S. Adams Rd.
Birmingham, Michigan 48011

Venture Investment Co.
925 N. Michigan Ave.
Saginaw, Michigan 48602

Minnesota

First Midwest Capital Corp.
110 S. Seventh St.
Minneapolis, Minnesota 55402

Minnesota SBIC
2338 Central Ave., N.E.
Minneapolis, Minnesota 55418

Northland Capital Corp.
402 W. First St.
Duluth, Minnesota 55802

Northwest Growth Fund, Inc.
960 Northwestern Bank Bldg.
Minneapolis, Minnesota 55402

Retailers Growth Fund, Inc.
5100 Gamble Dr.
Minneapolis, Minnesota 55416

Mississippi

Sunflower Investment Corp.
Int. of U.S. Highway 49W
Indianola, Mississippi 38751

* M indicates a Minority Enterprise SBIC.

Vicksburg SBIC
302 First National Bank Bldg.
Vicksburg, Mississippi 39180

Missouri

Atlas SBI Corp.
1808 Main St.
Kansas City, Missouri 64108

Capital for Business, Inc.
P.O. Box 13184
Kansas City, Missouri 64199

Equilease Capital Corp.
4647 Hampton Ave., Suite 102
St. Louis, Missouri 63109

Montana

Capital Investors Corp.
Capitol Bldg., Suite C
Missoula, Montana 59801

Small Business Improvement
Co.
711 Central Ave., P.O.
Box 1175
Billings, Montana 59103

Nevada

J & M Investment Corp.
647 W. 3rd St.
Reno, Nevada 89502

New Hampshire

Massachusetts Capital Corp.
1838 Elm St.
Manchester, New Hampshire
03104

SCI Tronics Fund, Inc.
43 Spring St.
Nashua, New Hampshire
03060

New Jersey

Capital SBIC
143 E. State St.
Trenton, New Jersey 08608

Engle Investment Co.
35 Essex St.
Hackensack, New Jersey 07601

Main Capital Investment Corp.
818 Main St.
Hackensack, New Jersey 07601

Monmouth Capital Corp.
First State Bank Bldg.,
P.O. Box 480
Toms River, New Jersey 08753

Monmouth Capital Corp.
P.O. Box 335
Eatontown, New Jersey 07724

Prudential Minority
Enterprises (M)*
213 Washington St., Box 594
Newark, New Jersey 07101

Rutgers Minority
Investment Co. (M)*
18 Washington Pl.
Newark, New Jersey 07102

SBIC of Eastern States
1438 U.S. Route 130
Cinaminson, New Jersey 08077

* M indicates a Minority Enterprise SBIC.

New Mexico

New Mexico Capital Corp.
1420 Carlisle, N.E.
Albuquerque, New Mexico
 87110

New York

15 Broad Street Resources
 Corp.
15 Broad St.
New York, New York 10005

Bancap Corp.
420 Lexington Ave.,
 Room 2352
New York, New York 10017

Basic Capital Corp.
40 W. 37th St.
New York, New York 10018

Beneficial Capital Corp.
10 East 40th St.
New York, New York 10017

Bonan Equity Corp.
60 E. 42nd St., Suite 2530
New York, New York 10017

Broad Arrow Investment
 Corp.
Route 55 Ft. Hunter Road
Amsterdam, New York 12010

Broadway Capital Corp.
41 E. 42nd St.
New York, New York 10017

Canaveral Capital Corp.
26 Court St., Suite 902
Brooklyn, New York 11201

Capital for Technology Corp.
75 E. 55th St., Suite 601
New York, New York 10022

Capital for Future, Inc.
635 Madison Ave.
New York, New York 10022

Central New York SBIC
738 Erie Blvd. East
Syracuse, New York 13204

Central New York SBIC
1231 Main St.
Buffalo, New York 14209

Central New York SBIC
56 N. Main St.
Rochester, New York 14604

Central New York SBIC
1056 Broadway
Albany, New York 12204

Chase Manhattan Capital
 Corp.
1 Chase Manhattan Plaza
New York, New York 10005

CMNY Capital Co., Inc.
77 Water St.
New York, New York 10005

Communications Fund, Inc.
1271 Avenue of the Americas
New York, New York 10020

Conresco Corp.
444 Madison Ave.
New York, New York 10022

Creative Capital Corp.
99 Park Ave.
New York, New York 10016

---

* M indicates a Minority Enterprise SBIC.

Criterion Capital Corp.
10 Fiske Pl.
Mount Vernon, New York
  10550

Diversified Realty Funding
  Corp.
299 Park Ave.
New York, New York 10017

Empire SBI Corp.
57 W. 57th St.
New York, New York 10019

Equilease Capital Corp.
270 Madison Ave.
New York, New York 10016

Equitable Life Enterprises
  Corp. (M)*
1285 Avenue of the Americas
New York, New York 10019

Equitable SBI Corp.
350 Fifth Ave.
New York, New York 10001

Esic Capital, Inc.
420 Lexington Ave.
New York, New York 10017

Excelsior Capital Corp.
115 Broadway
New York, New York 10006

Fairfield Equity Corp.
295 Madison Ave.
New York, New York 10017

First of Orange County Corp.
178 Grand St.
Newburgh, New York 12550

FNCB Capital Corp.
399 Park Ave.
New York, New York 10022

Franklin Corp.
1410 Broadway
New York, New York 10018

Globe Capital Corp.
221 W. 57th St.
New York, New York 10019

Great Eastern SBI Corp.
230 Park Ave.
New York, New York 10017

Hamilton Capital Fund
660 Madison Ave.
New York, New York 10021

Hemisphere Capital Corp.
100 Merrick Rd.
Rockville Center, New York
  11571

The Hanover Capital Corp.
485 Madison Ave.
New York, New York 10022

Intercoastal Capital Corp.
18 E. 48th St.
New York, New York 10017

Inverness Capital Corp.
345 Park Ave.
New York, New York 10022

Investor Enterprises, Inc.
295 Madison Ave.
New York, New York 10017

Kent Capital Corp.
530 Morgan Ave.
New York, New York 11222

* M indicates a Minority Enterprise SBIC.

Lake Success Capital Corp.
5000 Brush Hollow Rd.
Westbury, New York 11590

M & T Capital Corp.
One M & T Plaza
Buffalo, New York 41240

Midland Capital Corp.
110 William St.
New York, New York 10038

Mid-Atlantic Fund, Inc.
2 Pennsylvania Plaza
New York, New York 10001

Minority Assistance Corp.
  (M)*
40 W. 40th St.
New York, New York 10018

Minority Equity Capital Co.,
  Inc. (M)*
470 Park Ave. South
New York, New York 10016

Multi Purpose Capital Corp.
31 South Broadway
Yonkers, New York 10701

New York Business Assistance
  Corp.
98 Cutter Mill Rd., Suite 235
Great Neck, New York 11021

New York Enterprise Capital
  Corp.
500 Old Country Rd.
Garden City, New York 11530

Nuclear Energy Capital Corp.
485 5th Ave., Room 1001
New York, New York 10017

Pioneer Capital Corp.
1440 Broadway, Room 1967
New York, New York 10018

Pioneer Venture Corp.
22 East 40th St.
New York, New York 10016

Preferred Capital for Small
  Business
16 Court St.
Brooklyn, New York 11201

Printers Capital Corp.
1 Broadway
New York, New York 10004

R & R Financial Corp.
1451 Broadway
New York, New York 10036

Real Estate Capital Corp.
111 W. 40th St.
New York, New York 10018

Realty Growth Capital Corp.
156 E. 52nd St.
New York, New York 10022

Royal Business Funds Corp.
250 Park Ave.
New York, New York 10017

SB Electronics Investment
  Corp.
120 Broadway
Lynbrook, New York 11563

SBIC of New York, Inc.
64 Wall St.
New York, New York 10005

* M indicates a Minority Enterprise SBIC.

Securus Corporation of
America
32 E. 57th St.
New York, New York 10022

Southern Tier Capital Corp.
219 Broadway
Monticello, New York 12701

Star Capital Corp.
76 Beaver St.
New York, New York 10005

Struthers Capital Corp.
630 5th Ave.
New York, New York 10020

Stuyvesant Capital Corp.
485 Madison Ave.
New York, New York 10022

Tappan Zee SBI Corp.
120 N. Main St.
New City, New York 10956

Union SBIC, Inc.
420 Lexington Ave.,
Room 2720
New York, New York 10017

Vanguard Capital Corp. (M)*
222 Westchester Ave.
White Plains, New York 10604

North Carolina

Cameron Brown Capital Corp.
4300 Six Forks Rd.
Raleigh, North Carolina 27609

Delta Capital, Inc.
320 S. Tryon St.
Charlotte, North Carolina
28202

Equilease Capital Corp.
2915 Providence Rd.
Charlotte, North Carolina

First Carolina Capital Corp.
20 S. Pack Square
Asheville, North Carolina
28807

Forsyth County Investment
Corp. (M)*
Pepper Bldg., Suite 305
Winston Salem, North
Carolina 27101

Hanover SBIC
411 S. College, P.O. Box 747
Charlotte, North Carolina
28201

Lowcountry Investment Corp.
West Vernon Ave.
Kingston, North Carolina
28501

Northwestern Capital Corp.
924 B Street
North Wilkesboro, North
Carolina 28659

Ohio

BRI Corporation
55 Public Square
Cleveland, Ohio 44113

Capital Funds Corp.
127 Public Square
Cleveland, Ohio 44114

Columbus Capital Corp.
100 East Broad St., 3rd Fl.
Columbus, Ohio 43215

* M indicates a Minority Enterprise SBIC.

Dycap, Inc.
88 E. Broad St., Suite 925
Columbus, Ohio 43215

Gries Investment Co.
922 National City Bank Bldg.
Cleveland, Ohio 44114

Karr Investment Corp.
1134 Corrugated Way
Columbus, Ohio 43201

Ohio Valley Capital Corp.
17th Floor Cent. Tr. Tower
Cincinnati, Ohio 45202

Union Commerce Capital, Inc.
Union Commerce Bank Bldg.,
    Room 111
Cleveland, Ohio 44101

Oklahoma

Alliance Business Investment
    Co.
11 East 5th St., Room 510
Tulsa, Oklahoma 74103

Bartlesville Investment
    Corp.
827 Madison Blvd., Box 548
Bartlesville, Oklahoma 74008

Capital, Inc.
2106 Liberty Bank Bldg.
Oklahoma City, Oklahoma
    73102

Equilease Capital Corp.
Room 202, North Building
Oklahoma City, Oklahoma
    73106

First Growth Capital, Inc.
5900 Mosteller Dr.
Oklahoma City, Oklahoma
    73112

Henderson Funding Corp.
2410 Plaza Prom Sheperd Mall
Oklahoma City, Oklahoma
73117

Investment Capital, Inc.
Main Street at Thirteenth
Duncan, Oklahoma 73533

Oklahoma Small Business
    Investment
4416 North Western Avenue
Oklahoma City, Oklahoma
    73108

Phillips Industrial Finance
    Corp. (M)*
257 Adams Building
Bartlesville, Oklahoma 74003

Superior Business Assistance
    Corp.
216 N.E. 40th St.
Oklahoma City, Oklahoma
    73105

Oregon

Cascade Capital Corp.
321 S.W. Sixth Ave.
Portland, Oregon 97208

Continental Investment Corp.
811 S.W. Sixth Ave.
Portland, Oregon 97204

---

* M indicates a Minority Enterprise SBIC.

Northern Pacific Capital Corp.
2300 S.W. First Ave.
Portland, Oregon 97201

Oregon SBIC
661 High Street, N.E.
Salem, Oregon 97301

Pacific SBIC
310 N.E. Oregon Street
Portland, Oregon 97232

San Francisco Pacific Fund,
   Inc.
812 S.W. Washington Street
Portland, Oregon 97205

Pennsylvania

Capital Corp. of America
121 S. Broadway St.,
   Room 610
Philadelphia, Pennsylvania
   19107

Capital for Technology Corp.
341 Fourth Ave.
Pittsburgh, Pennsylvania 15222*

Delaware Valley SBIC
Wolf Building
Chester, Pennsylvania 19013

Delaware Valley SBIC
1604 Walnut St.
Philadelphia, Pennsylvania
   19103

Equilease Capital Corporation
3 Parkway Center,
   Room 123 A
Pittsburgh, Pennsylvania
   15217

Fidelity America SBIC
113 South 21st Street
Philadelphia, Pennsylvania
   19103

Frankford Grocery SBIC, Inc
G Street & Erie Ave.
Philadelphia, Pennsylvania
   19124

Osher Capital Corp.
Twnsp. Line Rd. &
   Washington Lane
Wyncote, Pennsylvania 19095

Penna Capital Growth Corp.
1930 Chestnut St., Suite 307
Philadelphia, Pennsylvania
   19103

Penna Growth Investment
   Corp.
301 Gateway Two
Pittsburgh, Pennsylvania
   15222

Progress Venture Capital
   Corp. (M)*
1501 N. Broad St.
Philadelphia, Pennsylvania
   19122

SBIC of the Eastern States
1216 Arch St.
Philadelphia, Pennsylvania
   19107

Sharon SBIC
385 Shenango Ave.
Sharon, Pennsylvania 16146

---

* M indicates a Minority Enterprise SBIC.

Sun Capital Corp.
455 E. Bruceton Rd.,
   Box 10809
Pittsburgh, Pennsylvania 15236

Puerto Rico

Credito Investment Co., Inc.
1155 Ponce de Leon Ave.
Santurce, Puerto Rico

Popular Investment Co.
Banco Popular Center Bldg.
Hato Rey, Puerto Rico 00909

Rhode Island

Industrial Capital Corp.
111 Westminister
Providence, Rhode Island
   02903

Narragansett Capital Corp.
10 Dorrance St.
Providence, Rhode Island
   02903

Northeast Capital Corp.
111 Wayland Ave.
Providence, Rhode Island
   02906

South Carolina

Charleston Capital Corp.
134 Meeting St., P.O. Box 696
Charleston, South Carolina
   29402

Falcon Capital Corp.
89 Broad St.
Charleston, South Carolina
   29405

Floco Investment Company
Highway 52 North
Scranton, South Carolina
   29560

Low Country Investment
   Corp.
P.O. Box 10447 Rovers Annex
Charleston Heights, South
   Carolina

South Dakota

Berkshire Capital, Inc.
405 8th Ave.
Aberdeen, South Dakota
   57401

Tennessee

Financial Resources, Inc.
1909 Sterick Bldg.
Memphis, Tennessee 38103

First Cumberland Investments,
   Inc.
19 S. Jefferson, Room 204
Cookeville, Tennessee 38501

The Third's SBIC
Third National Bank Bldg.,
   3rd Fl.
Nashville, Tennessee 37219

Texas

Admiral Investment Co., Inc.
1302 Rusk Ave., Guaranty
   Building
Houston, Texas 77002

* M indicates a Minority Enterprise SBIC.

Alliance Business Investment
Co.
1010 Milam St., 2212 Tenneco
Building
Houston, Texas 77002

Brittany Capital Corp.
1600 Republic Bank Building
Dallas, Texas 75201

Business Capital Corp.
5646 Milton St., Suite 636
Dallas, Texas 75206

Capital Marketing Corp.
9001 Ambassador Row
Dallas, Texas 75222

Central Texas SBI Corp.
514 Austin Ave., P.O. Box 829
Waco, Texas 76701

Circle K Investment Corp.
900 Magoffin Ave.
El Paso, Texas 79901

CSC Capital Corp.
750 Hartford Building
Dallas, Texas 75201

Enterprise Capital Corp.
202 Central National Bank
Building
Houston, Texas 77002

Equilease Capital Corp.
3202 Wesleyan St., Room 212
Houston, Texas 77027

Equilease Capital Corp.
3505 Turtle Creek Blvd.,
Room 3504
Dallas, Texas 75219

First Capital Corp.
821 Washington
Waco, Texas 76701

First Business Investment
Corp.
Davis Building, Room 1320
Dallas, Texas 75202

First Dallas Capital Corp.
1401 Elm St.
Dallas, Texas 75202

First Texas Investment
Company
506 Nebraska St., P.O. Box
495
South Houston, Texas 77587

First Texas Investment
Company
P.O. Box 341, 120 Jefferson
St.
Sulphur Springs, Texas 75482

First West Texas Capital
Corp.
305 First National Bank Bldg.
Odessa, Texas 79761

Northwestern Investment Co.
First National Bank Bldg.,
Drawer F
Levelland, Texas 79336

Providence SBIC
4100 W. 51st St., Box 607
Amarillo, Texas 79109

Republic SBIC
Republic National Bank Bldg.
Dallas, Texas 75201

---

* M indicates a Minority Enterprise SBIC.

Rice Investment Co.
3200 Produce Row
Houston, Texas 77023

SBIC of Houston
640 W. Building
Houston, Texas 77002

South Texas SBIC
121 S. Main St., Box 1698
Victoria, Texas 77901

Tarrant Capital Corp.
800 Main St.
Ft. Worth, Texas 76102

Techno Growth SBIC, Inc.
2701 Grauwyler Rd.
Irving, Texas 75060

Texas Capital Corp.
Lincoln Liberty Life Bldg.
Houston, Texas 77002

Texas Equity Corporation
215 Cotton Exchange Bldg.,
   Box 1704
Dallas, Texas 75201

Trammell Crow Investment Co.
2720 Stemmons Freeway
Dallas, Texas 75207

UCC Venture Corporation
1 Brookshollow Plaza,
   Room 1008
Dallas, Texas 75247

United Business Capital, Inc.
1102 South Broadway
La Porte, Texas 77571

West Central Capital Corp.
P.O. Box 412
Dumas, Texas 79029

Western Capital Corp.
2123 First National Bank
   Tower
Dallas, Texas 75202

Utah

Intermountain Capital
   Corporation of Utah
18 West 3rd South Street
Salt Lake City, Utah 84101

Utah Capital Corp.
2510 South State St.
Salt Lake City, Utah 84115

Virginia

Capitol Area Investors, Inc.
3701 Chain Bridge Road
Fairfax, Virginia 22030

Capitol Area Investors, Inc.
4023 Chain Bridge Road
Fairfax, Virginia 22030

Investment Funds, Inc.
P.O. Box 12300
Norfolk, Virginia 23452

Metropolitan Capital Corp.
2550 Huntington Ave.
Alexandria, Virginia 22303

Reba Investment Co.
147 Granby Street, Room 338
Norfolk, Virginia 23510

SBI Corporation of Norfolk
1216 Granby St.
Norfolk, Virginia 23510

Security SBIC
4023 Chain Bridge Rd.
Fairfax, Virginia 22030

---

* M indicates a Minority Enterprise SBIC.

Tidewater Industrial Capital
  Corporation
207 Granby Street
Norfolk, Virginia 23510

Tidewater SBI Corporation
746 Granby St., P.O. Box 479
Norfolk, Virginia 23510

Tidewater Industrial Capital
  Corporation
T.F. 22 Mil. Circle Shopping
  Center
Norfolk, Virginia 23502

Virginia Capital Corporation
808 W. United Virginia Bank
  Building
Richmond, Virginia 23219

Washington

Capital Investors Corp.
Old National Bank Building,
  Suite 1005
Spokane, Washington 99201

Equilease Capital Corp.
217 Pacific National Bank
  Bldg.
Bellevue, Washington 98004

Futura Capital Corp.
4218 Roosevelt Way, N.E.
Seattle, Washington 98105

MESBIC of Washington, Inc.
  (M)*
3300 Rainier Ave., South
Seattle, Washington

Northwest Business Investment
  Corporation
929 West Sprague Ave.
Spokane, Washington 99204

SBIC of America
1910 Fairview Avenue East
Seattle, Washington 98102

Trans-America Equity, Inc.
1021 Westlake Avenue North
Seattle, Washington 98109

Washington Capital
  Corporation
106 N. 2nd Ave., P.O. Box
  1517
Walla Walla, Washington
  99362

Wisconsin

Capital Investments, Inc.
735 North Fifth St.
Milwaukee, Wisconsin 53203

Commerce Capital Corp.
6001 N. 91st St.
Milwaukee, Wisconsin 53225

Commerce Capital Corp.
106 W. 2nd St.
Ashland, Wisconsin 54806

Commerce Capital Corp.
126 Grand Ave.
Wausau, Wisconsin 54401

Commerce Capital Corp.
9 South Main
Fond du Lac, Wisconsin 54937

* M indicates a Minority Enterprise SBIC.

First Wisconsin Investment
   Corp.
735 N. Water St.
Milwaukee, Wisconsin 53202

Growth SBIC, Inc.
811 E. Wisconsin Ave.,
   Suite 940
Milwaukee, Wisconsin 53202

Rec. Business Opportunities
   Corp. (M)*
316 Fifth St.
Racine, Wisconsin

Wisconsin Capital Corp.
840 N. 3rd St.
Milwaukee, Wisconsin 53233

---

* M indicates a Minority Enterprise SBIC.

Index

1 2 3 4 5 6 7 ← P Y → 9 8 7 6 5 4